# HERBS

# Rodale's Home Gardening Library™

# HERBS

### edited by Anne M. Halpin

 **Rodale Press, Emmaus, Pennsylvania**

Book design by Marcia Lee Dobbs and Julie Golden
Illustrations by Frank Fretz and Kathi Ember
Photography credits: Rodale Press Photography Department: photos 1, 3, 4, 6, 7, 8, 9, 11, 12, 13; Pat Seip: photos 2, 5, 10

**Library of Congress Cataloging-in-Publication Data**

Herbs.

    (Rodale's home gardening library)
    1. Herb gardening.   2. Organic gardening.   3. Herbs.   I. Halpin,
Anne Moyer.   II. Series.
SB351.H5H374    1988     635'.7       87-23310
ISBN 0-87857-735-1   paperback

  2   4   6   8   10   9   7   5   3   1   paperback

# Contents

**Chapter 1:**   Designing an Herb Garden . . . . . .   1

**Chapter 2:**   Growing Herbs  . . . . . . . . . . . . .  15

**Chapter 3:**   25 Favorite Herbs to Grow . . . . . .  30

# 1
# Designing an Herb Garden

**H**erbs are easy to grow and require less time and attention than most other plants. They are relatively immune to insect attack, and in some cases provide protection for other plants in the garden.

The added pleasure of the fragrance they provide can't be overlooked. The hovering sweetness of lavender seems to float over and around other scents in the garden. Rosemary's spicy aroma makes the air fresh and clean. Few things are more delightful than the scent of creeping thyme trodden upon, or the fresh, cooling fragrance of mint or lemon balm brushed against in passing.

An herb garden can be formal or informal, geometrical or naturalistic; it may be on level ground or hilly terrain, large or small, but the basic principles of garden design should be observed in order to achieve the desired effect.

The garden area may incorporate a terrace or other level space to unite house and garden, an expanse of lawn, or groundcover, with beds or borders for the planting of a flat terrain, or a series of multilevel terraces and slopes on a hilly plot.

Contrast is an important element in garden design. It can be achieved through size divisions and material used, through use of color, light, and shadow. Proportion, mass, and perspective are just as important in a harmonious and beautiful garden design as they are in a painting on canvas.

Every garden has a mood, either by design or by accident. Be

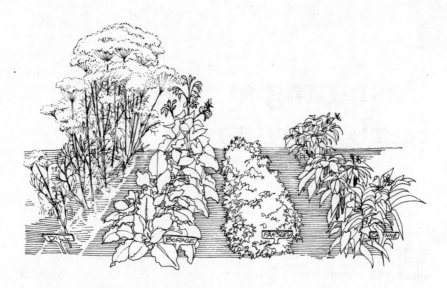

One way to plant an herb garden is in rows like the vegetable garden. This garden contains a row each of dill, borage, parsley, and cayenne.

it ever so subtle, an emotional response is evoked by the vista presented the viewer. The formal garden presents a mood of stately dignity—an expanse of low-growing plants or lawn, framed with a precise hedge, bordered by tall trees or shrubs arranged in perfect symmetry and balance. The beautiful geometric patterns of Renaissance herb gardens are a classic example of formality in garden design.

Gracefully drooping willow boughs reflected in a quiet pool, surrounded by a delicate green carpeting of sweet woodruff, create a scene of quiet tranquility. This is a very different herb garden.

Flowering herbs in a sunny border, with their bright splashes of color, create a mood of gaiety, while the deep-shaded greenery with sounds of water spilling over rocks can provide the peace and coolness of the deep forest within the garden boundary.

You may want to landscape your entire home with herbs, or you may wish to plant herbs only in a selected area. There are several elements to the whole herbal landscaping project. One should consider the borders, the groundcover, and the trees and shrubs; you may begin your landscaping experience with any one or all of these elements. Too, you must decide, before you go too far, whether you want an overall design that is formal or informal, contemporary or traditional. You may even want to consider a rock garden or a wild garden.

In the following pages, you'll find information on each of the landscape elements and on creating a design suited to you and

This delightful backyard landscape holds healing herbs in many unexpected places. In the foreground a flower bed includes peony, sage, and elecampane; marjoram, thyme, and oregano grow in the crannies in the stone wall; and the grove beyond is home to birch, basswood, and other healing trees.

your home. Your eyes will be opened to some new and exciting ways in which herbs can complement your environment.

## The Perennial Border

The herbaceous bed or border is a flexible feature and can be used to beautify a variety of areas in the garden—a space between

Flowering herbs can make a delightful border for a flower bed near the back door. This garden includes borage, calendula, and yarrow.

hedges and lawn, a corner between garage and wall, or any other location that would benefit by a decorative planting.

For an attractive border, flowering from spring through fall, materials should be carefully planned. Consider decorative effect, size, habit, color, texture, blossoming season, and fragrance. Hardiness and adaptability to soil conditions are also important. Plants requiring moist shade cannot be planted alongside sun-loving varieties if they are to thrive.

Taller plants should go in the back, the dwarfs in the foreground, and the intermediates throughout the rest of the area. Arrange for interesting contrasts in foliage and pleasing combinations of color, and have a few fragrant ones within easy reach for a pinch of their scented leaves as you go by.

Here is where we find many favorite herbs—tall mullein in purple, red or yellow; veronica in shades of pink, lavender, or blue; red valerian or brilliant monarda with its long season of scarlet flowers; tall clumps of white, daisylike feverfew; and in yellows there are ferny tansy with little buttonlike flowers, rue with its blue-green foliage, daisy-flowered arnica, silvery cinquefoil, and adonis. And no herb garden could be complete without lavender.

An edging may be desired, especially in the more formal designs. Silvery fringed wormwood and dark opal basil are good for foliage contrast. Germander can be clipped into a neat hedge. Neat patches of fragrant thymes are always welcome.

The perennial border or bed has been called the "lazy man's garden" because, if carefully prepared, it requires a minimum of attention for a beautiful display. Perennials can be expected to last for many years; therefore the bed should be well prepared prior to planting. If drainage is a problem, the area should be dug out and a layer of coarse gravel and sand placed at least 2 feet below the soil surface. The planting soil must contain a good amount of humus, well-rotted manure, and about 10 pounds of bone meal for every 100 square feet, all thoroughly mixed.

A prepared bed, well mulched, requires a minimum amount of watering and weeding. Proper watering is important. Too much water will produce leggy plants, lacking aroma and flavor. Spraying just the soil at ground level will have a tendency to bring roots upward and keep them close to the surface, where they can easily dry out. Watering must be thorough to reach deeper roots. Give the plants enough water to produce puddles on the surface, then don't water again until it is really needed. With a deeply developed root system, plants can stand long dry periods without damage. Morning watering is best, especially during warm, close weather, since damp foliage overnight may encourage and spread fungus diseases. A mulch over winter is usually adequate protection, and for lusty spring growth, a topdressing of compost is beneficial.

## Groundcovers

Groundcovers provide many interesting possibilities in creating pleasant little garden scenes within the landscape design. They can be used to define various areas by contrast of form and color. A groundcover may be the best solution for an area too small for the lawn mower, or too shaded for a satisfactory lawn. Groundcovers are used to beautifully cover dry banks or steep slopes and help prevent erosion.

Chamomile can replace grass and will take mowing. Creeping myrtle *(Vinca minor)*, a broadleaf evergreen, does very well in shaded areas, and sweet woodruff also likes shade. Ground ivy *(Nepeta hederacea)*, related to catnip, is a hardy perennial that rapidly forms an attractive mat in either shade or open situations. Low-growing thymes and veronica can be used in small areas. Ajuga, available in several colors of foliage, thrives in shade or sun. The woodland garden might have wild ginger or trailing arbutus spreading under the trees.

For hilly banks, slopes, and other large or dry areas, prostrate rosemary, uva-ursi, or low-growing junipers can be planted. Pennyroyal and fringed wormwood can become borders, while creeping thyme and corsican mint will fill in the crevices in the walkways. In short, there's an herbal groundcover to suit most any situation or location.

## The Formal Garden

The formal garden, large or small, begins with a design that must proceed from the dwelling. The doorway or walkway will set a line from which the design can flow. Almost any geometric form can be used: it may be a square or rectangle, divided by a cross of walks which may or may not have a central feature, such as a sundial, fountain, or statuary where they cross. The four lesser squares or rectangles can be broken into smaller parts, separated by smaller walks.

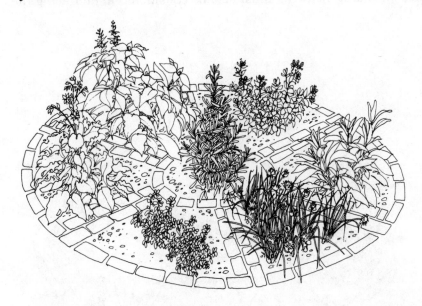

A circle is a classic herb garden design. This garden has beds of marjoram, rosemary, basil, sage, chives, oregano, and borage, with pathways of brick defining each area.

A circular pattern may be used, with walks radiating from the center like the spokes of a wheel. Designs may be adapted from some of the early medieval gardens where the geometrics used formed a knot at the focal point of the pattern.

For a formal garden, symmetry and perfect balance are essential. Elements of equal size and weight balance each other. They should be neat, trimmed, and precise. Plants are grown within the beds formed by the walks. Lower-growing plants are placed adjacent to the central walk, with taller varieties radiating outward. The varied symmetrical forms of coniferous evergreens make them adaptable to the formal garden, as backgrounds, borders, and accents. Shrubs and plants with irregular growth habits will need pruning or symmetrical arrangement when used in formal groupings.

The variety of texture, mass, and color available in herbs creates interesting contrasts and gives definition to the overall design. These elements must also be considered in producing the

If your taste runs more to neatly structured shapes, you might want to create a formal garden of geometric beds. Carefully trimmed hedges define the beds in this garden. Formal herb gardens are quite elegant, but require meticulous tending to maintain their neat, precise look.

symmetry and balance required. The formal garden is usually bordered by a trimmed hedge. Individual beds may be defined by neatly trimmed, low-growing plants.

The choice of plants is governed by individual taste or preference, climate, and availability. However, the essential materials for the traditional formal herb garden should include the "great herbs," as they were called. These are balm, basil, bergamot, hyssop, lavender, lovage, sweet and pot marjoram, mint, rue, sage, and spike vervain.

For year-round beauty, perennial herbs can form the framework of the garden, allowing areas for annuals to be planted in their season. Carefully plan the arrangement of plants according to size, texture or mass, and color. Arrange foliage colors to provide interesting contrasts, silver-gray against reds or bronze, dark greens to accent variegated or golden-green colors.

Some of the low-growing plants with woolly silver or gray foliage are antennaria, betony or lamb's ears, dittany-of-Crete, and woolly thyme. The low-growing artemesias, fringed or silky wormwood, and silver mound are feathery, gray-green; santolinas have finely divided foliage of the same hue but coarser than the artemesias. Dwarf sage and French thyme are also low-growing, with gray-green foliage. Among the taller plants of this coloring are horehound, the lavenders, marjoram, mugwort, sage, and Roman wormwood.

Deep greens can be found in English thyme, germander, green santolina, rosemary, white yarrow, and winter savory. Rue has a definite blue-green coloring.

For shades of red or bronze, use bronze ajuga as a low-growing groundcover, purple or dark opal basil for an area of medium height, and bronze fennel for a tall, background effect.

Variegated leaves can be found among the scented geraniums. Dwarf variegated sage leaves are gray-green and white with accents of purple. Variegated mint leaves are green and yellow, with a reddish stem; pineapple mint, green edged with white. Golden thyme has gold-tinged leaves in winter and spring; silver thyme leaves are green, edged in silvery white. Both of these are low, upright thymes. Golden lemon thyme is a creeper with golden green leaves. Most of the other culinary herbs are in the medium green color ranges.

Plants that lend themselves to clipping into hedges include gray and green santolina, germander, hyssop, lavender, and southernwood. By careful selection of appropriate herbs the garden can be as colorful and harmoniously designed as a Persian carpet.

## Contemporary Herb Gardens

For a house of contemporary style, garden designs often feature paved areas and patterns with distinct angles and curves, worked out by use of beds containing plants and various combinations of crushed rock, bark, and pavings. Plantings are based on tone, texture, and form of the plants. The object of interest or specimen plant is placed off-center, balanced by a larger area of subdued importance. Within the boundaries of the garden may be divisions, perhaps only one or two, or several. These functional divisions are planned and arranged, somewhat like the rooms of a house, into areas for various activities. Each is a separate area, yet together they form a harmonious unit.

Areas for outdoor living and dining should flow out from the house, becoming an integral part of the dwelling itself. Shade here might be provided by a wide-branching sweet birch or slippery elm. Groundcovers of varying textures and colors can set off larger plantings. Bronze ajuga, blue-flowering vinca, or the creeping thymes and mints are effective. Service areas can be attractively screened by a group of fast-growing poplars, broom, or elder. The exotic flowering passion vine or twining hops with papery yellow clusters on attractive wood-framed supports can also provide a division or screen.

The possibilities of the garden's area should be carefully studied. The enthusiastic desire for as many varieties as possible can sometimes result in overcrowding and a cluttered effect. Reasonable restraint, discrimination, and a sense of scale and proportion are needed to achieve the clean, quiet, functional beauty required by contemporary design.

## The Informal Garden

All things that are found in formal gardens are suitable for use in informal design, the difference being in the manner in which

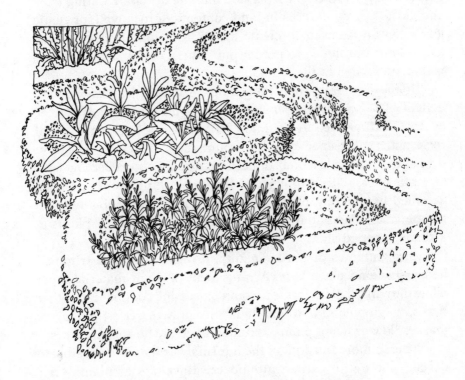

Herb garden beds can be created in free-flowing, informal shapes.

they are arranged. Rather than the symmetrical relationship seen in the formal plan, the informal garden is casual in effect, yet by no means does it come into existence accidentally, without planning; it must be carefully ordered and worked out, bringing into mutual relationship the various characteristics of the garden situation. Informal does not imply an unkempt wilderness or jungle conditions.

The formal garden can be designed with compass and ruler, but the art in informal design is one that conceals the design. It requires strict discipline applied in such a manner that the resulting effect is graceful charm and ease.

The individual peculiarity of each garden situation will suggest the way it can be incorporated into the design. Existing trees and shrubs, irregularities in land contours, a rock wall, or rustic fence can all be used to create a design of unique beauty. The transition from house to garden must be a uniting link—all elements are related to the whole.

In the informal garden, there is the intrigue of the unexpected—delightful, apparently unplanned features, arranged so as not to be evident until arrived at. It might be a delightful arrangement of rocks with tiny creepers growing around them, fresh-scented lavenders and delicate blossoms, or perhaps a small pool reflecting light airy branches, with bright green arbutus trailing over the banks, accented by a clump of tall, reedlike equisetum nearby. A small stepping-stone path may lead to a wild garden of natural plants in a shady, wooded area.

Straight rows of border plants, precise beds, and trimmed hedges have no place here. Arrangement of plant material must allow the natural plant forms to complement and contrast each other into satisfying combinations; light airy growth set off by darker masses, low-growing plants accented by a few flowering spikes.

There's more freedom in the informal garden. It is possible to develop the entire garden around certain kinds of plants—not necessarily to the exclusion of all others, but rather in a manner that will emphasize the importance of the chosen ones.

Although less maintenance is required for trees and shrubs than in the formal arrangement, removal of dead and unruly growth, pulling of weeds, thinning and replanting of perennials, as in any garden, are definite requirements. Order and discipline are just as important as in the formal garden; the significant difference is that they are not so apparent.

## The Wild Garden

Suitable materials for a wild garden are dependent upon the area in which the garden is located. In its truest sense, it is a collection of ecologically correct plants, native to the area. A wild garden of cacti and desert plants would not be appropriate for the seashore, nor would a collection of bog plants be suited to the prairie.

Naturalized clumps of herbs form a semiwild herb garden in a sunny meadow. This garden includes clumps of mustard, chicory, mugwort, and mullein.

In planning a wild garden, a study should be made of the plants in their natural state, observing their locations and choice of companions, in order to create a similar environment in the garden. In many areas where forest conditions still prevail, or at least once existed, a wild garden can be worked out which will appear as a piece of untouched woodland. Whether it occupies a large area, or just a tiny planting at the foot of an evergreen, it must not look planted, but rather as if it had been there all along. And to look natural, it must be planned that way.

Good drainage is important and must be checked and attended to at the outset. Woodland plants require soil very rich in humus. Large amounts of compost, leaf mold, and aged manure are needed. Proper shade must be provided, whether it be the dense shade of evergreens, or the light midsummer shade of a deciduous tree. Plants should be set out in colonies—groups of one species growing together. Colors and varieties should not be mixed. A natural, harmonious arrangement that provides interest and accent is accomplished through careful planning and design.

## Obtaining Plants for the Garden

Many herbs and native plants can be purchased at nurseries. In most areas, there is at least one grower who specializes in collecting and propagating the natives that can be adapted to the garden environment. Your local nursery may be able to direct you to one. Be sure to have the proper botanical name for the plant you desire. A request for stagbrush, or cramp bark, might result in a blank stare, but if you ask to see the viburnums, a group of plants would probably be presented for your selection. There may be several common names for one plant, and several different plants may have the same or very similar common names, but there is one proper botanical name for each plant. Seeds may be available from various specialty seed suppliers by mail.

# 2
# Growing Herbs

Often, when the question of physical requirements for herbs is brought up, people are unable to distinguish between herbs on one hand and other plants like vegetables and fruits on the other. Herbs throughout the centuries have remained "simple" plants, fully expressing their characteristic individualities simply because man has left them alone and did not subject them to rigorous selection and breeding programs. Unlike vegetables they have not been bred for quantitative growth, and hybridization is nearly absent. A visitor from the Egypt of 3,000 years ago would still recognize a coriander plant growing today in our garden.

The ability of herb plants to hold and reproduce their original characteristics over thousands of years helps us today in answering questions of physical requirements for these plants. The first step is to determine the natural habitat or environment of the specific herb. The more the climate in which we grow it resembles that of its home region, the more ideal are the climatic conditions. Since in general most herbs originate from the areas around the Mediterranean and north, we are safe to assume that a similar climate would make our herb plants feel at home and grow without much trouble. Thus the great majority of herbs prefer a climate with a great amount of sunshine, low humidity, seasonal changes, and an even distribution of an average amount of rainfall.

## Soil Requirements

Herbs are modest creatures, quite often pioneer plants which make use of the smallest amounts of nutrients a soil can offer and still thrive well and look healthy. Lavender, for example, or chamomile and thyme are able to flourish where other plants would make a very poor showing. Though there are exceptions to this rule, the majority of herbs feel comfortable in a well-drained soil of sandy, even gravelly, structure. This does not mean that they would not do well in other soils, but drainage remains always an important factor. For the purpose of a home gardener, every type of soil can actually be prepared without great effort to accommodate any herb that he or she desires to grow.

## Soil Preparation

Obviously, different herbs prefer different types of soil and soil conditions and consequently need specific soil preparation. So particulars about individual herbs are discussed in Chapter 3. There are, however, some initial requirements for successful herb growing that apply to all herbs.

### Drainage

Drainage describes the ability of a soil to handle the water from rainfall or irrigation. The ideal type of soil is expected to absorb any normal amount of rainfall within a reasonably short time without leaving excessive water for run-off. A soil which is able to meet these expectations is said to have good drainage. A soil having problems ingesting all water from rainfall, and thereby causing run-off, is said to have poor drainage.

The reasons for poor drainage are varied. It can be a sign of low organic matter content because organic matter, primarily in the form of humus, can absorb a great amount of water. The home gardener would do well to add a high amount of manure compost over a period of years until the organic matter content has been improved.

Some gardening areas never seem to produce impressive growth. Drainage is poor; the rain runs off, and during a dry period the soil becomes a dry powder. Plants even begin to wilt unless artificially watered. Closer investigation will usually reveal a rock formation or layers of shale or rock a foot or more below the topsoil. The water-holding capacity of this type of soil is rather limited, and plant roots are confined to the few inches of top soil. Here improvements will be achieved by breaking up the subsoil, removing the rocks, and replacing them with topsoil. Should this be too cumbersome or expensive, the only other solution would be to start a garden in a more ideal location.

In preparing an area for herbs, another requirement should be kept in mind as an important part of soil preparation. Quite a number of herb seeds are small and slow to germinate, while another group of herbs, especially all the thymes, grow close to the ground and hardly reach a height of more than 2 inches. For both groups it is mandatory to grow them in soil that is as weed-free as possible.

Weeds should be discouraged by an early working of the soil. Prior to planting the soil can be hoed, raked, tilled, or cultivated at weekly intervals, thus preventing sprouting weed seeds from getting established. Plowing or spading the garden in late fall aids in weed control and prepares a fine seedbed for spring planting. The pulverizing power of the frost works to benefit the fine seeds of thyme, marjoram, and others which can be seeded outside if the soil preparation allows it.

To make gardening easier, especially rototilling and seeding, all stones larger than a small egg should be picked up. Whatever stones will pass through the spaces of a rake may be considered harmless.

## Fertilizers

Most herbs don't require lots of fertilizer. They thrive on soils enriched simply with manure and compost.

Herbs respond quite well to fertilization with compost; in

fact, long experience has shown that compost is the ideal fertilizing agent for all herbs, though the stage of breakdown in the compost pile at time of application can vary with the specific plants. For the home gardener and all-purpose use, the compost should be made from a variety of materials (manures, leaves, weeds, kitchen garbage) and should be well decomposed. In the North, it takes about a year to finish a compost, including two turnings. Less time is required in warmer areas. Detailed information on composting can be found in books devoted to the subject, or books on organic gardening methods.

Apply compost in the spring, after spading or plowing the ground. It should be worked into the soil by cultivation, hoeing, or tilling within a day. If planting does not immediately follow, it is advisable to till or work the soil once more before setting out the herbs, thereby destroying young weeds that have germinated in the meantime and at the same time helping to distribute the compost more uniformly throughout the soil.

## Mulching

There is no question that herbs should be mulched. The first and foremost reason is to keep the leaves of the herb plants clean in case of heavy rains. Parsley and oregano, for example, grow so low that whole plants can be blown over in a strong storm and pushed into the soil. A mulch will prevent this.

Another reason for mulching, of course, is weed control. In stands of vegetables or flowers, weeds are a nuisance; in herbs, however, weeds are much higher and faster-growing than the low herb plants and would actually choke out the herbs if not controlled. Herbs need sun and light and moving air around them, all things that weeds would deny them. Mulching becomes a tool of the gardener to deny the weeds the conditions which would allow them to germinate and grow without an effort. The most effective way is to cover the soil with several inches of mulch material soon after planting.

A final benefit of mulching is its ability to preserve soil moisture. Evaporation from the soil is extremely low because the mulch material is shading the soil continuously. Furthermore, the impact of the falling rain or irrigation water is broken by the mulch, and the water gently led to the soil, where shallow roots can immediately receive it.

As far as mulch materials go, each herb grower has his or her own favorites, partly chosen on the basis of availability. Among the most popular herb mulches for home garden use are cocoa hulls, grass clippings, chopped hay, chopped straw, and chopped seaweed.

Cocoa hulls are ideal, because they keep little water for themselves and are high in nitrogen. A mulch material influences soil temperatures to a great degree by shading the soil and keeping it cooler than it would be without a mulch. However, a dark mulch material, like cocoa hulls, absorbs rather than reflects the sun's warmth. Herb plants like a warm soil, especially thymes and rosemary.

The other mulch materials are well known to organic gardeners and are generally easier to get. They are handled the same way they would be for vegetables, except the thickness of application should be less for herbs. Chopped material is preferred because it settles better, looks neater, and is less prone to interfere with harvesting.

## Plant Propagation

The next step for the practical herb grower is planting. Like all plants, herbs can be propagated from seeds, cuttings, divisions, and to a lesser degree, layering.

### Herbs from Seeds

Starting herb seeds indoors is easy. There are just a few rules to follow. If you're starting seeds indoors for later transplanting, begin no earlier than March; otherwise plants will get spindly and weak, or fall prey to insects and disease. Each variety should be seeded in a separate container to allow for varying germination times. Garden cress, for example, germinates within 48 hours, while lavender might take three weeks.

Seeds are sown in rows *without* covering them; the seeds should remain exposed to the air. Rows should be at least 1 inch apart and about ¼ inch deep, the growing medium itself 1 inch below the rim of the container. After the seeds have been thinly sown in the row or rows, water with a fine mist and cover the container with two sheets of newspaper; then place it in a warm area, preferably 70°F or a little warmer. From then on, the seeds need misting about three times a day.

First choice for a growing medium should be finely milled sphagnum moss, straight or mixed with crushed granite. Or substitute finely screened, aged compost mixed with equal parts of crushed granite. Bear in mind that seeds started indoors do best in a growing medium which has hardly any plant nutrients.

Once the seeds develop their first leaves, which should happen in seven to ten days, they need to be transplanted either into 2¼-inch pots, one to a pot, or into flats with a minimum spacing of 1¼ inches. At this stage each little plant should have a single root, which may be tipped for easier transplanting. Set the plant itself into the soil deeper than it grew in the seed flat to encourage side-root formation. The medium can be a regular potting soil or at least a richer medium than that of the seed flat.

After four weeks the plants will be ready for transplanting into 3-inch pots and from there, after another three to four weeks, may be planted outside anytime the weather permits.

## Herbs from Cuttings

Some herb plants have to be propagated from stem cuttings, either because the plants don't form seeds or because the seeds don't grow true to variety. In addition, some herbs which could be started from seed are easier and faster to propagate from cuttings.

The rooting medium for cuttings can be a variety of substances; again the choice is an individual one. A mixture of equal parts of milled sphagnum moss, crushed granite, and finely screened aged compost or humus is a good medium to start with. Some cuttings, especially pennyroyal, also do quite well in Jiffy-7 growing pellets, which upon addition of water expand into little potlike objects held together by polyethylene netting.

A cutting is actually a term used for the sprig which is cut off the tip of a branch, and for our purpose it should be about 3 inches long. Starting at the bottom, remove the leaves with a sharp knife to within 1½ inches from the top. The prepared cutting is then ready for the final cut and planting.

The final cut of the prepared cutting should be made with a sharp knife by cutting, not pressing, with a downward stroke through the stem at a slight angle. Leave about 1 inch of bare stem. This finished cutting should be planted in the well-packed growing medium in 2¼-inch pots, a flat, or a special growing area set aside for cuttings. A uniform soil temperature of at least 65°F should be maintained and the cuttings misted several times daily to prevent wilting. After about three weeks they should have formed enough roots to be transplanted into individual pots or shifted from the 2¼-inch pots to 3-inch pots. Planting the herbs outside is determined again by variety and weather conditions.

## Herbs from Divisions

Dividing mature plants as a means of propagation and rejuvenation is an old practice which also can be employed for herbs. Of course, it works only if the herb grower already has an old plant. Dividing plants is the easiest method of plant propagation. In general, the spring is the best time of year for division. The individual plant is dug, the soil shaken off, and the clump either pulled apart or carefully separated. Each section of plant with a good amount of roots is then treated as an individual plant. Sometimes one clump will give up to a dozen new plants.

## Herbs from Commercial Growers

Many small local herb gardens have sprung up around the country and should be able to supply at least the more common varieties of herb plants. Some growers will also ship herb plants by mail. The best time to plant most herbs outdoors is May or early June, with the exception of a few hardy plants which may be planted in April or even earlier.

At local herb gardens ask the grower to dig plants in the field, and carry the herbs straight home and plant them there. They'll need little care because their growth will be in harmony with the season and accustomed to the weather.

## Indoor Culture

There's no need to forego the companionship of fresh herbs once winter sets in. Many herbs can be brought indoors, and with proper care, survive the winter months easily. Proper care simply means providing enough light and moisture, a good climate—not too hot or cold, with a daily breath of fresh air—and room for growth.

August is not too early to begin selecting the plants you want to move indoors. The first step is to assure yourself that you have a window that gets sufficient light. While direct sunlight is to be most prized, it isn't absolutely necessary, and some herbs don't like direct sunlight anyway. But most herbs do like sun, and the window that gets at least five hours of direct sun each day is the best for your indoor herb garden.

Your next task is to select containers. All sorts of pots are available, in plastic, clay, and terra-cotta, and you can make or buy boxes of redwood and cedar. Just make sure the container provides enough room for the roots of your herbs. The common rule of thumb is to use a pot with a diameter of one-third to one-half the final height of the plant.

Any good organic potting medium will serve. You can use the mixtures of milled sphagnum moss, ground granite, and finely screened compost mentioned earlier in this chapter. Just remember that not all herbs desire fertile soil, and conduct your potting accordingly.

Herbs can be simply transplanted from the garden to the pot, or new plants can be started from a cutting or from seed. Probably the most foolproof technique is to transplant a healthy plant from the garden.

Select a proper size pot. The drainage hole in the bottom should be covered by stones, a bit of broken crockery, or a layer of sphagnum moss to prevent the soil from blocking the drainage area. Partially fill the pot with potting soil. Hold the plant in position, with the roots spread naturally. Add more potting soil, tamping it firmly with your fingers. When you are finished, the surface of the soil should be about ½ inch below the rim in small pots, and about 1 inch from the rim in pots 6 inches or more in diameter. If you put too much soil in the pot, your herbs won't get enough moisture when you water; too little soil and your herbs may drown.

When the plant is in the pot, thoroughly water it and leave it outside for several days, permitting it to establish itself. Move the potted plant indoors before the first frost.

Once indoors, the potted herb should be kept in the sunny spot you've selected. Don't shock your plant with a cold draft—herbs like a temperature of 50° to 70°F. Never let it get above 75°F. Herbs also like fairly high humidity, and since most home heating systems provide dry heat, you'll do well to frequently water the plants and spray the foliage. These humidity measures will keep the herbs healthy and pest-free. Should pests invade, you can hand-pick the pests or spray them with soapy water. An occasional dose of weak liquid fertilizer will keep the herbs well-nourished.

## Harvest and Storage

Don't wait until the last days of summer to think about how to preserve your herbs. Not only will you work yourself silly trying to get them all dried or frozen before the first killing frost, but you'll have missed the prime harvesting time for most herbs. A little planning and thought at the season's beginning will enable you to make the best use of your herbs.

There are several ways to preserve herbs. The method you choose will depend upon what you want to use them for and when they'll be ready for harvest. Most herbs you'll want to dry; but some you can freeze or refrigerate. And if you move your favorite culinary herbs to the windowsill in the winter, you'll be able to use them fresh all year.

Herbs for culinary use are usually ready to harvest just before flowers appear on the plant. At this time, the plant contains the most oils and the greatest flavor and fragrance.

Herbs for drying should be harvested early in the season so that successive cuttings can be made. Harvesting perennial herbs late in the season reduces flavor and increases the chances of plant loss as well. Plants need the chance for regrowth in order to survive the winter. Another caution is not to cut annuals such as basil and borage too close to the ground. The lower foliage is necessary for continued plant growth. At the end of the season the entire plant can be harvested.

The best time to harvest herbs is early morning, just as the sun dries the dew from the leaves, since the oils are strongest in the plants then. A chemical change takes place in the plants as the sun becomes more intense, and the oils diminish. It is best to do this harvesting on a clear day.

As soon as the herbs have been cut, waste no time getting them ready for drying. If the foliage is dirty, wash the leaves and shake off the excess water. If the plants have been mulched, it's not usually necessary to wash the plants before drying. This is especially important for basil, which bruises easily from too much handling. The tops and leaves can be picked off the heavier-stemmed herbs such as lovage and basil. Removing the leaves from the stems will shorten the drying time and provide better flavor and color. For herbs like parsley, leave most of the stems on until after drying.

## Drying

The most common method of drying herbs is also the most picturesque. The mention of herb drying inevitably conjures up visions of drying bunches of herbs hanging from an overhead nail.

A well-ventilated attic, shed, or barn can provide a suitable drying area for herbs, and a fan can be installed to increase air circulation.

To dry herbs this way, simply gather and tie them in small bunches. Hang them in a warm, dark place for about two weeks until they are dry. One drawback to this method is that the herbs sometimes get dusty. Each bunch of herbs can be put in a paper bag, then hung up to dry, but this variation extends the drying time by several weeks.

This latter method is good, however, for drying seed heads, such as anise, caraway, coriander, dill, and fennel. Care must be taken to avoid shattering the heads and scattering the seeds

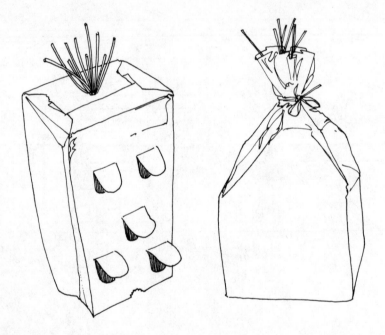

Two ways to dry herbs in paper bags: one that keeps off dust and one that saves seeds.

everywhere. The care begins with the harvest. The seed heads should be gathered in the early stages of ripening, just as the seeds turn from green to gray or brown. It should be done in the morning, just as the dew leaves the plants. Place the seed heads into a large paper bag or paper-lined basket, then clip the stems. When tying the stems, be sure to tie them into the neck of the sack so that they hang freely. Make certain that the seeds are perfectly dry before

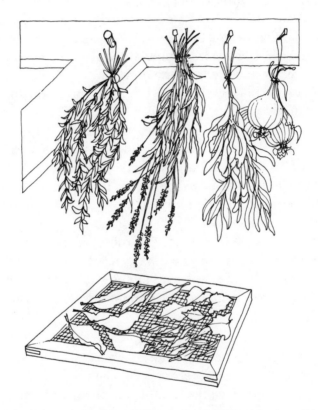

Herbs with volatile oils can be dried by hanging them upside down in bunches or by spreading the leaves in a single layer on a screen.

storing them since it takes seeds longer to dry than foliage; give them two to three weeks.

Another variation on air drying is to disassemble the herb plants and spread the parts on screens to dry. You can use a window screen or one constructed especially for the task. Prop it up to permit the air to freely circulate through the screen. Place it neither in direct sun nor in a damp spot.

The fastest method is oven drying at a temperature of 150°F or lower. Place herbs on sheets of brown paper that have slits cut in them to allow for the passage of air. With this method it takes from three to six hours to dry the foliage. After a few hours the leaves can be easily removed from the stems, then dried further, if necessary, to ensure complete drying before storing. Basil and chervil are very sensitive to heat, so a drying temperature of about 90°F is best to retain their color and prevent browning.

For storing the herbs dried by either method, an airtight container such as a glass jar should be used. The herb must be thoroughly dry before sealing in jars. Check after a few hours and then again after a few days to make sure that there is no condensation present on the inside of the bottle. Moisture indicates that there is still water present in the herbs. If the plants are not dry, remove from the bottle and redry.

Leave herb foliage whole when storing. The flavor is retained longer when whole leaves are stored. Crumble the leaves as you use them. Keep the dried herbs in a dark place to preserve the natural color. Sunlight will fade the leaves and destroy some of the flavor. Label all containers before storage to prevent later confusion.

## Freezing

Freezing is a simple way to store culinary herbs for winter use. Gather chopped or whole herbs, wash them if necessary, shake them dry, and then place them in plastic boxes or bags, properly labeled. Place these immediately in the freezer.

The herbs can also be blanched before freezing, although it's not necessary.

Don't defrost frozen herbs before you use them. If the recipe calls for minced herbs, it's easier to chop them while they are still frozen, since they break apart so readily. Chives, dill, lovage, mint, oregano, parsley, sorrel, sweet marjoram, and tarragon all freeze well.

Another way to freeze chopped herbs is to place them into ice cube trays filled with water. After freezing, place the cubes in a plastic bag, label, and store in the freezer. When needed, just pop an ice cube with herbs into soup, stew, or casserole.

## Fresh Storage

When storing fresh herbs in the refrigerator, harvest them as usual, place in plastic bags or special crisper boxes, and refrigerate. Herb foliage lasts longer if washed just prior to use rather than before it's stored. This method of storage is especially suitable in the late fall, so that fresh herbs are available for Thanksgiving and sometimes even for Christmas.

# 3
# 25 Favorite Herbs to Grow

T his chapter provides specific cultural information on 25 of the most popular herbs, along with tips on how to use them.

## Anise

Anise, an annual, grows from 18 to 24 inches in height. The first leaves are fairly large and wide, while the secondary leaves are featherlike. By midsummer, 2-inch clusters of tiny yellow-white flowers appear, followed in late summer by the gray-brown seeds for which the plant is generally cultivated. Each plant will have one to six umbrellalike clusters bearing six to ten seeds each.

The seeds are the most useful part of the plant, though the leaves can be used in cooking. The so-called aniseed is actually the fruit of the plant, and the seed is contained within the ⅛-inch-long kernel. Aniseed is easily dried by spreading it on paper or cloth in the sun or half-shade. Once dried, the seeds store well in tightly sealed containers.

The taste of the aniseed is sweet and spicy with a pleasant aroma. Its licoricelike flavor is added to cakes, soups, beverages, medicines, and mouthwashes, and its aroma to sachets and potpourris besides.

A bit of culinary lore from anise's past ties it to the tradition of the wedding cake. The Romans liked to finish off a big meal with a cake called *mustacae,* which was simply a mixture of meal and a number of savory seeds, including anise. The *mustacae* was meant to ease digestion and prevent flatulence. Since it was a custom to

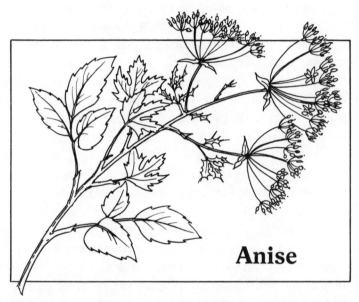

Anise is an annual herb that grows 18 to 24 inches tall with 2-inch clusters of tiny yellow-white flowers. The licorice-flavored seeds can be used in cakes, soups, and beverages.

conclude really big feasts (like a wedding meal) with a serving of *mustacae,* many lorists view it as the forerunner of today's wedding cake.

Anise is a stimulating condiment. A few seeds can perk up the taste of many a soup. Or try substituting aniseed for the cinnamon or nutmeg you add to applesauce. Mix a teaspoon of aniseed with a cup of cheese spread and spread on crackers for an interesting party or evening snack. Aniseed can also be added to almost any basic recipe for breads, cakes, or cookies. The stomach-warming seeds will brighten up many baked goods.

The leaves will add a fine aromatic taste to salads and dishes such as carrots if they are finely chopped and sprinkled sparingly over the food. A tea can also be made from the leaves.

Anise is a lovely garden plant, and easily grown. The seed needs 70°F warmth to germinate and the plant needs similar warmth for the seeds to ripen. A cool, damp summer can prevent you from getting a crop. It is, however, a short-season plant, and if you plant in May, the anise will probably clear the garden by August.

Since its long taproot makes transplanting a risky proposition, anise should be seeded wherever it is to grow. Sow the seed in rows, rather than broadcast, to ease the task of weeding, which will be necessary in the early weeks of growth. Cover the seeds with ⅛ to ¼ inch of soil; they should sprout in four to six days.

Anise is modest in its demands, and in fact doesn't like too much fertilization. Mulching may not be necessary, for anise's growing season is short and it grows tall enough to keep its leaves and flowers out of the dirt.

As the seeds ripen, turning from green to gray-brown, harvest them. The best time is the morning while the dew is still on them. Clip the seed clusters into a bag or container of some kind so the seeds are not scattered and lost. The leaves can be gathered discreetly throughout the growing season.

## Basil

Probably nowhere else in the herb world is there a plant with such a split personality as basil.

Although a favorite herb in today's kitchens, basil stands in the midst of a centuries-old controversy that, on one hand, attributes awful and evil powers to it and on the other, holds it an object of sacred worship.

Early Greek and Roman physicians believed that basil would thrive only if it were sown amid vile shouts and curses. That tradition gave rise to the contemporary French idiom *semer le basilic*—"sowing the basil"—for raving.

The Eastern sentiment toward basil, though, is one of unequivocal reverence. In its native India, the herb is hailed as a protector. Pots of basil are grown in temples, and it is believed that a home built where basil flourishes will be safe from all harm.

In Italy basil is a traditional sign of courtship. A beau is supposed to be able to guarantee the love of his lady by offering her a sprig of basil; a pot of basil on the balcony is a sign that the lady within is ready to receive her suitor.

And despite the French idiom spawned by basil, the French name for it is *herbe royale*—the royal herb.

Whatever basil's true mystical nature, it is one of the most widely known and used herbs in modern cooking. There is a bewildering profusion of varieties, the most common of which is sweet basil or garden basil.

As soon as the danger of frost has passed, sow basil seed in rows not more than ¼ inch deep. Or, if you're starting seeds indoors, transplant the young shoots when there is no longer any threat of overnight frost. Keep plants 12 inches apart.

Because basil likes a rich, weed-free, and well-aerated soil, beds should be cultivated thoroughly and treated with well-rotted manure or manure compost before planting. After sprouts appear, mulching will hold soil warmth and moisture and will discourage weeds. If the leaves curl downward during a dry spell, sprinkle the plant with lukewarm water.

After you take the first cuttings, the remaining growth will branch out to be ready for another trimming in two or three weeks. Harvesting can continue until the first frost, which usually kills the plants.

To prepare the leaves for storage, pinch them off at the stem and dry them in a well-ventilated, shady area. If they aren't dry within three days, finish drying in a low oven or the leaves will turn brown and black.

In the kitchen, basil imparts a delicious flavor to bland vegetables and soups, salad dressings, and egg dishes. For an interesting sandwich spread, add chopped basil to butter. Use basil on broiled tomatoes and in onion dishes. The French find it indispensable in turtle soup, and also use it widely in ragouts and sauces. Fresh basil leaves can even be cooked and eaten, spinach-style, as an aromatic vegetable dish.

Basil also can be preserved for winter use by soaking a few fresh leaves in vinegar. Fill a pint jar one-third with basil leaves, then add white vinegar, close the jar, and let it stand in the sun for three weeks. Or mash a double handful of fresh leaves in a 2-gallon crock of ceramic or stainless steel, then add a gallon of white or malt vinegar, and steep the same way. Boiling will shave one week off the steeping time.

## Bay

A storied medicinal and culinary herb, bay is probably most familiar as a plant grown for its looks, usually in big wooden tubs. It is indeed worth a special place in landscape design.

Left in its natural form, it is a lovely evergreen aromatic shrub, with elliptical, shiny, dark green leaves. It is slow growing, and when pruned and shaped as a tub-planted showpiece, bay seldom exceeds 10 feet in height. But in the South and in Mediterranean areas, bay trees have topped 60 feet. The bay is, however, very frustrating to grow from seed, and even using cuttings, the most popular method of propagation, will try your patience. The most reliable starting technique is to root a cutting, making sure you select a fresh, green stem. Be patient, since the cutting may take as long as six months to root. As a permanent growing medium, a moderate soil with good drainage will do. Bay likes sun, but needs protection from freezing temperatures and icy winds.

Bay leaves can be picked and dried the year round. The leaves have a delightful fragrance and are commonly used as seasoning for soups, stews, meat and fish, puddings and custards, and other foods.

The old herbalists saw bay as a virtuous tree. "They serve both for pleasure and profit, both for ornament and use, both for honest civil uses and for physic, yea both for the sick and for the sound, both for the living and the dead," wrote Elizabethan herbalist John Parkinson. Galen, the Greek physician, was quoted as recommending the leaves, berries, and bark as a diuretic and for liver ailments.

"Neither witch nor devil, nor thunder or lightning will hurt a man in a place where a Bay Tree is," said 17th-century herbalist Nicholas Culpeper. He may have overstated the case, but protective or not, the bay tree is worth the effort it takes to have, if only for its culinary and visual appeal.

## Beebalm

Beebalm is a part of America's history. An American perennial, it is the source of a tea which was a popular substitute for the imported variety among the mid-Atlantic patriots in the wake of the Boston Tea Party. That period was probably the best in beebalm's history, though it retains its mystique, thanks, perhaps, to a striking appearance and the richly American nickname of Oswego tea.

At least two of the plant's nicknames are derived from its showy flower. Both bees and hummingbirds are attracted by the blossoms, hence the name beebalm. The brilliancy of the scarlet-colored flowers has earned the appellations scarlet monarda and red bergamot. The leaves are dark green, growing 4 to 6 inches long. The plant has a dense, rather shallow root system with many runners, making root division a most reliable method of plant propagation.

Among the foremost growers of beebalm in the United States were the Shakers, who had a settlement near Oswego, New York. The Shakers were great herbalists; they valued beebalm not only for its tea and its other culinary uses, but also for its medicinal virtues. An infusion of beebalm is supposed to be good for colds and sore throats. The leaves can also be used to flavor apple jelly, fruit cups, and salads.

The entire plant emits a strong fragrance similar to citrus, but most like that of the tropical orange bergamot tree, hence the nickname bergamot. The fragrance contributes to beebalm's value as a garden plant, and makes it suitable for use in potpourris and other scented mixtures.

The most reliable way to start beebalm is to buy a plant. Plants from seed are very seldom uniform, since beebalm easily cross-pollinates with wild bergamot. What's more, it takes at least a year for plants grown from seed to establish themselves. Transplanting beebalm, on the other hand, works any time of the year except late fall. Once a planting is established, it should be divided every third year or it is apt to die out. The roots are easily pulled apart by hand. The center roots should be thrown out, and only the outer roots replanted.

Fertility, and especially the moisture-holding capacity of the soil, should be high. A sunny location is a further guarantee of healthy growth. Space clumps at least 2 feet apart. In late fall the entire beebalm area ought to receive a 1-inch covering of compost which will act as a winter protection and source of nutrients for the following year.

All herbs for tea can be used fresh and cut freely as needed, and beebalm is no exception. But beebalm needs a severe pruning, to within an inch of the ground, as soon as the lower leaves show signs of yellowing. The flowers will have barely formed at this stage. There are other harvesting variations. You can increase the size of the second-year bloom by sharply cutting back the plant before it blooms in its first year. Cutting back the stalk immediately after it blooms will generally promote a second, early autumn bloom. And you can harvest twice: once just before the plant flowers and again after it flowers; the teas made from the two harvests will differ, and some growers sell the two harvests as two different teas.

The best-quality tea material is achieved if the leaves are stripped off the square, hollow stems and dried in warm shade within two or three days. A longer drying period might discolor the leaves. When necessary, the leaves can be finished off in the oven at low heat.

## Borage

Borage is such a cheerful plant to have in your garden or potted by a sunny window that it isn't surprising to learn that it was prescribed 400 years ago for melancholy.

In the garden, borage is almost constantly in bloom and almost constantly surrounded by interested bees. In grows quite rapidly, spreading over a fairly broad area and self-seeding proficiently.

Borage is classified as a hardy annual. It grows 12 to 18 inches tall, but it isn't an erect plant, and a single healthy plant will spread over a 4-square-foot-area, covering it with hairy stems and leaves, brightening it with strikingly blue star-shaped flowers. Occasionally, a borage plant will bear both blue and pink flowers; the capacity to bear more than one color of flower at a time is characteristic of plants of the borage family.

Borage is believed to have originated in Aleppo, a city in northwestern Syria. An independent plant, it spread throughout Europe, where it remains a fairly common wild plant.

The young leaves are excellent in salads; the taste of borage is suggestive of cucumbers. The leaves may also be cooked and served like spinach. The leaves should be boiled with only a little water, then chopped finely and served with butter. The flowers are edible and their brilliant color makes them particularly decorative in the salad bowl. The flowers are often served candied (dip them in egg white, then sugar, and dry).

One of the oldest uses of borage blossoms is as a flavor-enhancing decoration in beverages. The Greeks and Romans floated the blossoms in their wine cups, but you can add them to cider, punch, lemonade, or other beverages. The leaves can be used to make their own beverage. Steeped in boiling water, borage makes a tea that soothes the throat.

Borage is quite easy to cultivate. It can be started from seed either indoors or in the garden. Whether seeded directly or transplanted, the plant should be given sufficient garden space to develop properly. It should be about 2 feet from any neighbors.

Once established, borage will self-seed, and offspring may well sprout around the parent plant before the growing season has ended. Although borage is relatively hardy, it shouldn't be seeded or set outdoors until the danger of frost is past.

Borage requires a fairly rich soil. A manure compost is the best fertilizer. The soil should be loose, well aerated, and hoed regularly to eliminate weedy competition. A mulch is a good idea, for borage likes a moist environment.

Borage is a nice plant to maintain in an indoor garden. It will thrive when given sufficient root space, a fertile potting medium, sunlight, and moisture. It has been said that a garden without borage is like a heart without courage. The same might be true for your windowsill.

## Calendula

Originally from southern Europe, the calendula or pot marigold is a hardy annual plant of the Composite family. It has light greenish yellow leaves and forms daisylike flowers in different shades of yellow and orange. The history of this herb is filled with poetry and symbolism, most of which has been in reaction to and appreciation of an unusual characteristic which has fascinated poets. At dawn, the moist calendula blossom opens with the rising sun, creating the poetic image of awakening. Its golden orange color brightens the day until sunset, when the early-to-bed marigold closes for the evening.

It was the Romans who recorded that the marigold was usually in bloom on the first day, or *calends*, of every month. From this observation, the Latin generic name *Calendula* was given to the herb.

In modern times, calendula has been used primarily as a local remedy with a stimulant effect. Calendula ointment is sometimes used as a dressing for small wounds. For relief from the pain of a wasp or bee sting, you might try rubbing a flower on the affected part.

In the kitchen, fresh calendula is primarily used in salads, whereas dried calendula adds a special touch to broths and soups. The taste of the leaves is at first pasty and sweet and then quite salty.

The seeds are unusual in shape and formation. Light yellow in color with at least a half dozen shapes ranging from winged to curled, the calendula seed stays viable for only a year; thus, fresh seeds are needed for each planting.

**Calendula**

Calendula, or "pot marigold," produces attractive flowers and tasty leaves that can be added to salads and soups.

Sometime in April or May, when the sun is shining, the seeds can be planted. The soil temperature should be at least 60°F for the seeds to germinate well. Although the plants need to be kept free of weeds and thinned out to stand 9 or 10 inches apart, there is not much more cultivation necessary in the care of pot marigolds. The different varieties offered by seedsmen usually represent various forms of double- or single-flowered plants with blossoms ranging in color from yellow to deep orange, the latter color being excellent for herb teas. In soil that is fairly rich, the flowers will begin to appear anytime from June to August. If you are interested in retaining a healthy flowering until early October, the phosphate content of your soil will be important. Although calendula may survive the first frost, a harder frost of 25°F will damage it.

As far as harvesting is concerned, most people are interested in the flower, which can be pinched off the stem. Each petal of the harvested flower head is pulled out by hand, leaving the green center of the flower. Because the only part of this plant generally used in food and medicine is the flower petal, it is considered to be a very expensive herb. The petals should be dried in the shade on paper rather than on screens, since once they are dried they have a tendency to adhere to the screen, making it difficult to remove them. They should also be kept from touching one another, since this can lead to discoloration. Marigold petals should be stored in a moisture-proof container to preserve color and flavor ordinarily lost in humid conditions.

## Caraway

Caraway is one of those utility herbs, a plant so pleasant and useful that it's among the best known and most widely used herbs in almost all parts of the modern world.

Its more obvious uses in the United States include flavoring rye bread and cheeses. Caraway has an enjoyable and distinctive licorice-flavored tang and has won sizable acclaim in kitchens throughout the world.

The plant is a biennial with feathery leaves similar to those of fennel and coriander, although caraway does not like to grow near fennel. It should be seeded directly into the beds where it will grow; it does not tolerate transplanting well. Because it is biennial, plant a new crop each year for a steady supply.

Seeding should be done in early spring for the full biennial cycle of the plant. Spring plantings will produce bushy green foliage, about 8 inches high, during the first summer. The foliage will retain its verdancy during the winter. During the second summer, 2-foot stalks topped by clusters of white flowers will develop. Seeds will form by midsummer and ripen by the fall. Harvesting time can be shortened if seeds are sown as soon as they're ripe in the fall. In the latter case, some seeds will be produced late the following summer.

Caraway should be harvested as soon as the seeds ripen and darken. Usually they can be separated from the umbel stems by threshing. Dry them in hot sun or over low stove heat.

Pay particular attention to weed control during caraway's early months. When the new shoots are about 2 inches tall, pinch out the smaller ones and allow the remaining plants 6 to 12 inches of room.

Fertilization is not critical, although caraway seems to prefer a fairly heavy soil on the dry side. Some herbalists recommend a planting of caraway to break up and aerate heavy soils.

Some companion gardeners plant peas and caraway in the same row. The peas come up first, and harrowing them in the normal way simultaneously controls weeds that hinder caraway's early growth.

The roots of the mature caraway plant are a delicacy that can be prepared and eaten much like carrots or parsnips. The leaves can be chopped and added to stews and soups and goulashes to lend caraway's tang to them. And caraway is said to aid the digestion of heavy starches such as cabbage, turnips, and potatoes.

Sometimes served as a side dish to dessert fruits, the seeds also can be added to cakes, puddings, and cookies. Use the seeds in apple dishes of almost every kind and in rye and black breads.

## Chamomile

Chamomile is an herb with a split personality, chiefly because it is really two plants though most people think of it as a single plant. The trouble is that German chamomile and Roman chamomile are two distinct plants with similar characteristics, but people familiar with one tend to think of it as the only chamomile.

The chamomiles are perhaps best known for their applelike fragrance and flavor, qualities which always come as a surprise to the uninitiated, for neither chamomile has any visual resemblance to an apple or apple tree. The applelike qualities, however, are strong enough to have earned the plants the name chamomile, which is derived from the Greek *kamai* "on the ground" and *melon* "apple" for ground apple.

Although the plants are generically different, their common characteristics are sufficient to confuse them in the minds of many. Both have daisylike blossoms, applelike fragrance, and foliage that could be described as feathery. Nevertheless, there are some distinguishing characteristics.

Roman chamomile *(Anthemis nobilis)* is a low-growing perennial, seldom topping more than 9 inches in height. It has finely divided leaves. The flowers have a large, solid central disk of a deep yellow color and creamy rays. The variety of best medicinal value has double flowers, but there is a variety with single flowers. The entire herb is strongly scented.

German chamomile *(Matricaria chamomilla)* is an annual with fine-cut foliage (though somewhat more coarse than *A. nobilis*) and a single daisylike flower with a yellow, hollow disk and white rays. The flower is smaller than that of *A. nobilis* and less strongly scented. The plant is erect, growing 2 to 3 feet tall. It has medicinal properties similar to that of *A. nobilis,* but regarding scent, it is of a lesser quality.

The most obvious difference between the two plants is that one is an annual, the other a perennial. Perhaps the most useful and pronounced distinction is the stature: Roman chamomile is nearly prostrate, while German chamomile is erect. The flower sizes are different, and the flower structure is different, one having a solid disk, the other a hollow disk.

Both plants are cultivated, but both escape cultivation at every opportunity and are occasionally found in the wild untended places of Europe and the United States. Both German and Roman chamomiles have been held in considerable esteem as medicinal

*(continued on page 51)*

Photos 1 and 2: In the garden, borage (above) is almost constantly in bloom, and usually surrounded by bees. Compact and hardy, chives (left) do well outside in the garden or in pots indoors.

Photo 3: Small pots of homegrown herbs make delightful gifts.
The small white pots on the table hold (left to right) dill,
basil, more dill, and thyme.

Photos 4 and 5: Beebalm (above) produces showy flowers and leaves that can be used to brew a flavorful tea. An herb garden planted in rectangular, timber-edged beds with brick paving between them (below) can make an attractive addition to any landscape.

Photos 6 and 7: A mixture of herbs can be planted as a border around a fence or garden path (left). Sage (below) is a hardy perennial that will withstand winters in most of the United States.

Photo 8: Adding dill, basil, borage, or other herbs to bottles of vinegar makes delicious and low-cost toppings for salads or marinades for meats.

Photo 9: This formal "knot garden" in New Jersey is made from carefully trimmed plantings of lavender, hyssop and other herbs.

Photos 10 and 11: Spearmint (right) is a versatile herb that can be used in juleps, sauces, and jellies. English lavender (below) looks equally beautiful in the garden and in dried potpourris.

Photos 12 and 13: Oregano (left) can be dried outdoors in the sun on warm fall days and packaged for later use. Fresh basil (below) makes a wonderful sauce for pasta, but it, too, can be dried and saved.

herbs. Both are particularly useful as tonics, being taken in the form of an infusion of the blossoms.

Roman chamomile is said to have, in addition to its tonic effect, stomach-strengthening, pain-relieving, and antispasmodic properties. An infusion of the blossoms is reputed to have a soothing, sedative effect, and has been used to calm the nerves and prevent nightmares.

Both chamomiles, of course, have served in more than a healing capacity. Chamomile tea, made from either herb, is a soothing beverage at any time, and it has some other uses too. It is an excellent rinse for blonde hair. It is also reputed to be an effective insect repellent; sponge it over the body, leaving it to dry on the skin.

Either chamomile is an excellent addition to the garden, but German chamomile especially can serve the gardener in more than an ornamental capacity. Chamomile tea is reputed to be an excellent greenhouse spray, serving to prevent a number of plant diseases, particularly damping-off.

The most reliable method of getting Roman chamomile is to purchase a plant (or several plants) and increase it by runners or root division. In some moist climates, it can be planted as an aromatic lawn.

German chamomile, an annual, has to be started from seed. The seeds are very tiny and of unpredictable viability. They have a germination rate of about 70 percent the first year and rapidly lose viability thereafter. Chamomile seed is one of the rare seeds that needs light for germination.

The most practical and successful method of starting the plants is to broadcast the seeds in early August, pack the soil lightly, and water until the little plants can be seen. By early September the plants will have developed enough to transplant to another location. No winter cover is needed as the plants are extremely hardy.

The seeds may also be started indoors in March and transplanted outside when large enough to handle, after they gradually were hardened-off, meaning exposing them to cold temperatures over a period of time, and not suddenly. Or they may be seeded directly in the garden after the danger of frost has passed. They should be sown in rows rather than broadcast.

## Chervil

Brought into Europe from the Levant and the shores of the Mediterranean, chervil is well known to gourmets as the basis of any herbal salad.

For centuries, this tasty herb has been an essential part of most English gardens, where it is said to have been introduced by the Romans. In southern Europe, it flourishes in the wild although it is native to Asia.

Many people call it "the gourmet parsley," since it has a more delicate flavor than parsley. It is used mostly to add zest to a salad, but the herb has a rich folklore and background in custom.

Pliny said that chervil was a fine herb "to comfort the cold stomach of the aged," and the boiled roots were thought to be a preventive against plague. In the Middle Ages, people used the leaves to soothe the pain of rheumatism and bruises.

The herb is best known for its use in salads, but it enhances soups, especially sorrel or spinach soup, and adds flavor to fish, eggs, meats, or vegetables.

There are two main varieties of chervil, plain and curly. The plants grow to about 2 feet in height, with small flowers arranged in umbels. The seeds look like tiny sticks, thin and about ¼ inch in length. Germination takes ten days or longer in the presence of light.

Start chervil from seed either indoors or directly outside as soon as the soil can be worked. Since the seeds require light for germination, they should not be covered with soil. However, too much light could dry out the sprouting seeds and kill them.

The best planting method is to make a furrow an inch deep, scatter the seeds evenly, and press them into the ground with the tines of a vertically held rake; water. Keep moist until the young plants are visible.

Because the plant grows quickly, indoor germination isn't as important as it is for other plants, and chervil's small, long root makes it more difficult to transplant than most herbs.

The plant should be sown in March or early April and after July for an autumn harvest. The chervil should self-sow generously. If some seedlings are lifted in late summer and put in a cold frame, they'll survive the winter there and in the spring, when the glass is removed, grow to more than 2 feet and become covered with blossoms. By putting some chervil in a cold frame, fresh leaves can be obtained all year.

Chervil thrives in cool weather, and thus does better early in the year and again toward the end of summer. In the middle of the summer it goes to seed without real leaf formation. It's possible to cut the leaves six to eight weeks after seeding. For a continuous supply of leaves, it's best to continually seed the plant throughout the summer, preferably in the shade.

The herb doesn't require much in the way of nutrients, and chervil can easily follow a crop that was fertilized with compost the previous year. Mulching with chopped hay or straw helps keep the soil cool and the plants clean.

The older leaves of chervil attain a horizontal position gradually, stop growing, and start to age. For this reason, the gardener should cut off these leaves first prior to their turning yellow. More leaves will develop from the center until the stalk pushes up, developing into a structure of flowering umbels.

Chervil is best used fresh. If you dry it, make sure it is stored away from light, since the herb will turn yellow or grayish in a short time if exposed to light. It will also pick up the slightest moisture above normal humidity and become stale.

# Chives

Hardy perennials, chives grow in clumps of small, white bulbous roots that send up hollow, green spears. The tender young spears are harvested and chopped or cut into small segments to grace a wide variety of dishes with their oniony flavor.

Because chives are difficult to store, many gardeners choose to maintain a fresh supply through indoor gardening.

Chives can be started from seed or purchased already started in young clumps. Seed should be sown as early as the soil can be worked, then covered with fine compost or sifted soil. Tap the covering lightly to assure good soil contact. The plants need rich soil, a fair amount of water, and full sun. Some gardeners border the garden with chives, which develop pretty bluish pink to lavender flowers.

Early mulching is wise to retain moisture and discourage grass and weeds, which are debilitating competitors for moisture and nutrients.

A fish emulsion fertilizer should be added to chives to replace nutrients, especially nitrogen, after repeated cuttings.

Chives are an encouraging project for a new herb grower because they develop quickly and produce in profusion. A bed of chives frequently produces more than a family can use, but even if that's the case, the tender green spears should be snipped close to the ground regularly to prevent the plants from becoming tough and to help the bulblets develop.

The root bulbs develop in clusters, which should be dug up, divided, and replanted every two or three years. Keep the new clusters 8 inches apart. A cluster of six bulbs is about right when dividing.

To bring a cluster of chives inside for the winter, transplant it into a 5-inch pot in late summer and sink the pot into the ground. After the first killing frost, mulch the pot or put it into a cold frame for about 90 days. Chives need this rest period to rejuvenate. Then bring the pot into the house, and put it in a sunny location. Give it water. Sometime in January, there will be a fresh supply of chives for harvesting.

The best way to preserve chopped chives is to freeze a glassful of them at a time.

Sprinkle chives in green salads and on tomatoes. Add them to sour cream or melted butter as a fine dressing for potatoes, or sprinkle them into soups, sausage dishes, and croquettes.

## Coriander

One of the most ancient of herbs still in use, coriander is known to have been cultivated in Egyptian gardens thousands of years before the birth of Christ. Coriander seeds were among the funeral offerings found in Egyptian tombs. And coriander spread early to Western civilizations, too; the great Greek physician Hippocrates used it in the fifth century B.C. There are several Old Testament references to coriander as an herb whose fruit is similar to the mysterious food, manna, that God showered upon the Israelites during their desert trek from bondage.

Coriander, though, is not so divine in all its aspects. The mature green plant, just before it goes to seed, emits a strong odor that some gardeners find highly offensive. Fortunately, that odor gives way to a pleasing aroma as the plant dries. The lasting odor of dried coriander has been described as a combination of sage and lemon peel.

The plant is an annual with slender, erect stems bearing finely divided leaves. It reaches a height of 1 to 3 feet. Coriander needs only moderately fertilized soil, but it cannot stand constant moisture. Because of its marked liking for well-drained soils and relatively dry climates, most of the commercially produced coriander is grown in arid areas of the world.

The seeds germinate in darkness. They should be planted outside in drills ½ inch deep and 9 inches apart. Because coriander prefers light, warm, and dry soil, a relatively warm and dry spring will give you a late April start. A less favorable season may cause you to wait until May for planting.

Coriander doesn't transplant well; sow it directly in its bed. If you do find it necessary to try a risky indoor start, plant in March and transplant in May. As much as coriander dislikes being near fennel, it welcomes anise as a neighbor and will benefit the formation of anise seeds.

Weed control is important while the early coriander fights to establish itself. By mid-August, it should be able to dominate its competitors, however, and even mulching should be unnecessary.

Coriander attracts a great variety of pollinating insects to the garden. The swirl of activity around it may alone be well worth all the trouble of growing coriander.

Harvest the coriander when the fruits turn light brown. The small globular fruits, which envelope the seed, are ⅛ inch in diameter, and will part into halves when they're dried and rubbed between the palms. It's this part of the plant that's most used in medicines and cooking. If the fruit balls aren't snatched at the right time, the fast-dropping coriander will reseed itself.

Coriander's commercial uses include the flavoring of foods and liqueurs and some confectionery uses, including the fortification of inferior-grade cocoa. The crushed fruit and seed are sometimes used in rich cakes, custards, and jellies. Along with the sugar-coated seeds of anise, caraway, and celery, coated coriander fruits are used in multicolored cake sprinkles to decorate baked goods.

This herb imparts a wonderful spiciness to sausage and red meats. In pickles and beet salads, it makes a different and tasty addition.

## Dill

Dill is a hardy annual plant that resembles fennel in many ways. Like fennel, dill develops a spindly taproot, although dill roots are not usable. Dill also develops a round, shiny green main stem like fennel, but while fennel commonly shows many stems from a single root, there's seldom more than one on a dill plant.

Dill is prolific and if a few plants are left to seed themselves, a gardener will have his entire next season's supply without replanting.

The plant likes moderately rich, loose soil, and full sun. Because young plants are difficult to transplant, start dill outdoors in rows ¼ inch deep, or by broadcast sowing, or in drills 10 inches apart. Cover the new seeds with a light soil blanket. Germination takes place in 10 to 14 days at about 60°F.

Both leaves and seeds are used. If plants are to be harvested before going to seed, plan successive replantings from April through mid-July. For pickling — dill's major culinary use — seeding should be done in early May.

Leaves are harvested about eight weeks after seeding, with the outer leaves cut first, always close to the stem. If you do not use the leaves fresh, dry them within a day or two, in the shade, by placing them on a fine screen or on paper. Use a low oven to complete the drying, if necessary, for dill leaves will lose their color and flavor if drying time is prolonged. Seal them in a tight jar. Freeze them fresh as an alternative to drying.

Plants left to mature will grow 2 to 3 feet tall, develop the familiar flower-tipped umbels, and eventually go to seed.

For pickling, harvest the flowering umbels and a few leaves. To harvest the seeds, wait until they're light brown, then cut the umbels, dry them in the sun a few days, and shake loose the seeds.

Small amounts of dill may be sown in the corners of the vegetable garden and allowed to mature and bloom for honeybees. Dill is a good herb to grow with cabbage, and, when lightly sown, with carrots, cucumbers, lettuce, and onions. It should never be allowed to mature when sown with carrots, for it has a severely depressing effect on them at this late stage.

Dill's culinary uses range from seasoning cheeses and creamed dishes to flavoring vinegar. (Dill vinegar is easy to make. Simply soak a small amount of dill leaves in vinegar for a few days.) In France, dill is used to flavor cakes and pastries. More likely, you'll want to add its chopped leaves to soups and salads. Creamed chicken, potato salad, and plain cottage or cream cheese take on a tangy snap with the addition of a few chopped leaves. Try it on steaks and chops, too.

## Lavender

Lavender is so well known that its name is instantly associated, not only with the delicate sweet fragrance of its oil, but with the specific purple hue of its tiny petals. Lavender supports one of the largest herbal industries in the world, with centers of cultivation for commercial use being England and France.

There are three basic species of lavender, and each has several varieties. Most widely known in America is English lavender (*Lavandula vera*), also known as true lavender because its oil is of the highest, most fragrant quality. That quality also makes it the most highly valued for commercial production, although spike lavender (*L. spica*) produces a greater volume. French lavender (*L. stoechas*), has an odor that's "more akin to Rosemary than to ordinary Lavender," in the words of Mrs. Grieve, an early twentieth-century herbalist.

To determine which variety to grow in your garden, decide whether the main object will be the flowers or the leaves. If it's the flower you want most, then English lavender is your plant. For leaves, the spike lavender will produce a broader leaf and more oil.

All the lavenders are shrubby perennials. English and French lavenders prefer sandy, coarse, even rocky soils that are warm and moderately fertilized. They all like a sunny location.

Because all the lavenders are natives of the warm Mediterranean climate, they may be difficult to establish in American gardens. English lavender, though, should fare the best; it is the hardiest of the three varieties.

Leaves of all the species are light green-gray, somewhat resembling in shape those of rosemary. English lavender carries the narrowest leaves; French and spike lavender have broader leaves.

Flowers of the famous lavender color form in June and July in spikes at the top of the plant. French lavender flowers tend to be a darker shade than those of the other species.

Seeds, which form later in the season, are a shiny dark grayish brown and generally rather difficult to germinate. They take up to four weeks to sprout, and they have a very low percentage of survival. Lavender started from seed should be planted inside in February because of its long germination time.

Or, lavender can be started by taking August cuttings, which will form productive young plants by the next spring. English lavender winters best of the three species, but all should be afforded some protection against killing frosts. A southern exposure would help, and a windscreen is a necessity.

The lavender spot in the garden should be neutral to alkaline in acidity. Mulching is not necessary, in fact not even desirable, for it lowers the soil temperature to the discomfort of the plant. Fertilizing is of minor importance, but if the soil is so devoid of nutrients that it just has to be enriched, use only well-rotted compost or manure, never fresh.

Harvesting time for leaves is not critical, but flowers must be taken just before they open. They lose their aromatic properties quickly after opening. Both flowers and leaves are dried in shade at 90° to 100°F. They dry well and pose no storage problems.

One of lavender's finest uses today is in sachets and pillows to perfume linen. Said to repel moths, flies, and mosquitoes, a folk formula for making a room-sized insect repellent is to absorb a few drops of lavender oil on a cotton ball, then suspend it from the ceiling.

The dried flowers alone, sewn into a linen pillow, can be tucked among dainty linens to impart to them a lovely fresh scent. For lavender water, add a drop of musk and an ounce of lavender oil to 1½ pints of mild white wine. Shake well, leave to settle for a few days, then shake again and pour into airtight bottles. Or add 2 ounces of refined essence of lavender to 1½ cups of good brandy for a powerful concentrate of lavender water.

A pleasant lavender vinegar is made by mixing six parts of rosewater, one part spirits of lavender, and two parts of vinegar. Or steep fresh lavender tops in vinegar for a week, shaking the mixture each day. At the end of the week, filter the lavender vinegar and store it in airtight bottles.

## Lemon Balm

Lemon balm, named because its crushed foliage smells like lemons, is not only fragrant and useful but is also very prolific and easy to grow. A native of southern Europe, it can sometimes be found growing wild in the United States and England.

Lemon balm is a fairly hardy perennial. The root system is short but dense, and the stems square and branching. The plant seldom grows more than a foot tall indoors, but may reach 3 or 4 feet outside. Its leaves are heart-shaped or broad ovals, yellowish green, and covered with stiff hairs on the top surface.

Lemon balm can easily be started from seed. If left alone, the plant will reseed itself in the garden. It can also be started in a greenhouse or in pots in the house. To start the seeds indoors, press them into fine, friable soil. When the seedlings are an inch tall, thin them to 2 inches apart. When they have reached 4 inches, they can be set out. Allow 2 feet between plants on all sides.

Cuttings and root divisions are also easy ways to start lemon balm. Root divisions can be made in the spring or fall by dividing the roots into small pieces with three or four buds to each piece. Plant the pieces 2 feet apart. If you're making your root divisions in the fall, allow plenty of time for the plants to become established before the first serious frosts.

Lemon balm should be planted in fairly fertile, friable soil in partial shade. Although the plants will grow in sunlight, they will do much better in the shade. Allow 2 feet on all sides between plants, since they tend to spread sideways. Weed until the plants are well established. An early mulching with hay or straw will prevent the herb from becoming too soiled.

Water during dry periods to guarantee continued growth of the plants and prevent yellowing of the leaves. In the fall, cut off all decayed growth from the roots. Although the roots are hardy, mulching with pine or spruce branches or leaves during the winter will greatly improve chances of survival.

Harvesting lemon balm is easy, and you may get as many as three cuttings a season. Lemon balm should be harvested before it flowers for optimum fragrance, although a good deal of its scent will be lost in even the most careful drying. To harvest, cut off the entire plant 2 inches above the ground. Be careful to avoid pressure of any kind if packing the herb in boxes or cartons, and try to avoid bruising either the stem or the leaves when you are harvesting the plant.

Balm should be carefully dried within two days of picking — it has a tendency to turn black unless it is dried quickly. Do not harvest if dry sunny weather is not predicted for several days. Drying is most effectively done in the shade at temperatures between 90° and 110°F. It's best to use trays or sieves for drying the herb, rather than tying it in bunches on a string. If you plan on using your lemon balm for tea, dry both leaves and stems.

Lemon balm is attractive to bees — as the early Greeks recognized. In fact, its present scientific name is derived from the Greek word for "bee."

Balm tea can be made by pouring a pint of boiling water over 1 ounce of the herb. Infuse the blend for 15 minutes, cool, and strain. You may wish to add honey or lemon peel. The tea is used by herbalists to induce perspiration and cool patients who have fevers.

Lemon balm has culinary uses as well. Leaves can be added to salads or to fruit compotes for a pleasant, subtle flavor. A few leaves will improve the taste of a cup of tea.

## Marjoram

Of nearly 30 varieties of marjoram, sweet marjoram is without a doubt the most popular among herb gardeners in the United States.

Several varieties share many characteristics of the herb commonly called oregano. In a few cases, the common properties are so close that confusion reigns over whether the plant is a marjoram or an oregano.

Sweet marjoram is a tender perennial in its native Portugal and similar Mediterranean climates, but in North America it's impossible to keep the plant alive through even the mildest winter. So consider it an annual that must be started anew from seed each year.

The dense, shallow root system of sweet marjoram can utilize no more than the top few inches of soil, and so a fairly rich humus is desirable. The plant's square stems grow upright to about 12 inches. Stems are surrounded by a profusion of branches bearing oval, slightly fuzzy leaves with short stems. White or pink flowers appear in midsummer but are almost entirely covered by small leaves that form a little ball at the end of each stem.

Because the seeds are so small, it's almost impossible to tend them properly outside. So sweet marjoram should be started indoors in March in flats. Pat the seeds lightly into well-sifted soil, which should be kept moist. Transplant when the soil has warmed.

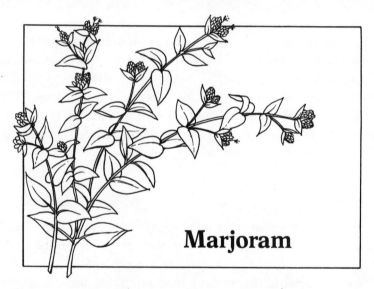

## Marjoram

Marjoram is a sweet culinary herb that can enliven many meat, pasta, or vegetable dishes.

Outside, the plants should be spaced 6 to 8 inches apart, although they can be placed in three-plant clumps if the shoots are still small. Five such clumps should provide enough sweet marjoram, both fresh and dried, for a year's use. Weeds are fierce competitors with young marjoram; keep them under strict control if they're evident during marjoram's slow early growth.

Aged compost—never fresh manure—should be used. Regular hoeing is essential to control weeds; in fact, this plant can be "hoed to maturity" and will respond to hoeing in the same way that other plants respond to heavy fertilization. For that reason, mulching should be delayed until two weeks before the first harvest. The ideal mulch is cocoa hulls followed by chopped hay or straw.

The first harvest comes at the time the green ball-like flower buds appear at the ends of the stems, although for early use some young shoots may be pinched off. When flowers appear, the whole plant should be cut back to an inch above the ground to stimulate a second growth. That second growth, lush and fuller than the first, is really the main crop. Cut the plants again when flower heads form the second time.

For drying, place the cut plant on a fine screen or on paper and put it in a warm, dry, shaded area. When dry, rub the plant through a fine screen. Leaves will powder and sift through the screen; the woody stems will remain behind. Sweet marjoram, unlike some other herbs, retains its full flavor when it's dried.

Traditionally, sweet marjoram has been a symbol of youth and beauty and happiness. An early literary tribute to marjoram was paid by Virgil who, in his *Aeneid,* wrote of being "where the sweet marjoram, breathing its fragrance, surrounds him with flowers and soft shade." The French, too, cherished the sweetness of the herb. It was customary in France to tuck a few sprigs of it away in hope chests and drawers of linen.

In the kitchen, use marjoram with green vegetables, turkey, pork, lamb, or eggs. Potpourri, too, is enlivened by this tangy herb, whose fresh tops are sometimes added to home-brewed beer for an unusual snap. Sprinkle a few cut-up leaves of fresh marjoram on lightly buttered whole grain bread and broil it slightly for flavorful herb toast.

## Mint

The mint family, Labiatae, is large, having about 160 members including basil, horehound, hyssop, lavender, lemon balm, marjoram, rosemary, sage, thyme, and many other familiar herbs in addition to the plants we call mints. But the true mints are the many examples of the genus *Mentha,* the best known of which are spearmint and peppermint. Other mints include the apple mint, Corsican mint, curly mint, orange mint, water mint, and dozens of other species, varieties, and odd hybrids.

As members of the same genus, the mints share a common background and some common characteristics. All mints have square stems and opposite leaves. Most are rampantly spreading perennials which inhabit moist, rich-soiled areas throughout the world.

The name *Mentha* was first connected with the mint plant by the Greek philosopher-scientist Theophrastus more than 300 years before Christ. Mintho, the story went, was a beautiful nymph who was loved by Pluto, god of the underworld. Persephone, who had been abducted by Pluto to reign with him over his domain, became jealous and changed Mintho into a fragrant and lowly plant which to this day waits at the shady edges of Pluto's dark world. The plant, of course, is the mint.

The mints can be used in preparing fragrant baths and as ingredients in potpourris, sachets, and other fragrant bags. A room can be scented simply by hanging a bunch of mint in a doorway. This is a common practice in India and other hot countries, for the fragrance lends the impression of coolness.

It is impossible to pinpoint a single most common use of mint. Mint tea, mint jelly, and mint sauce are all everyday commodities. But there are some relatively uncommon ways to use mint. Mix chopped mint leaves with cream cheese and spread it on whole grain bread. Mix a cup of chopped leaves in a salad, tossing it well, and dress it with oil and vinegar. Fresh green peas can be perked up by stirring 2 tablespoons of minced mint into each quart of the vegetable. The ingenious cook can find a variety of dishes that benefit from a dash of mint.

Clearly, peppermint, *Mentha piperita,* is the most versatile of the mints. It can be used in many of the culinary applications already described, and it has a history of medicinal use. It has been listed for more than 140 years as an official drug plant. Used in a variety of compound medicines, it often serves only to make disagreeable preparations palatable. Of itself it has antispasmodic action. Most herb books list it as a stimulant, stomach aid, and gas reliever.

Peppermint has a shallow root system and seems to channel all its rooting energies into the formation of runners which form below and, more abundantly, above ground. The pointed, oval leaves are attached to square stems of a purplish green color which extend to the undersides of the leaves.

The only sensible way to establish a good peppermint bed is to purchase a plant or two. Peppermint has been selected for oil content and flavor and is reproduced vegetatively to retain the desired strains. Though peppermint seed germinates well, it must be remembered that plants do not come true from seed.

Peppermint requires a soil of good fertility and tilth, high moisture-holding capacity, and free of weeds, especially grasses or clovers. The spacing of individual plants should be at least 2 feet because the runners will fill in this distance within one year. As soon as the runners begin to spread, hoeing has to be entirely replaced by hand weeding. Mulching can be done only in a thin layer in order not to interfere with the development of the shoots which grow out of the nodes of the runners or stolons. The main purpose of the mulch material in this case is to keep the plants clean. Up to three cuttings are possible each year. After the final harvest in fall, all exposed roots and runners are best covered with a 1- to 2-inch-thick layer of compost or well-rotted manure. This will protect the plants from frost damage and at the same time fertilize the peppermint for the following year.

The time for harvesting is judged by the flowering tendency and the yellowing of the lower leaves. As soon as either or both stages have been reached, the entire plant, including the shoots of runners, is cut 1 inch above the ground. No stems with leaves should be left after the harvest because they could become hosts for disease.

The best quality peppermint is achieved by stripping the leaves off their stems, and drying them whole in warm shade.

Spearmint, *M. spicata,* while somewhat less potent than peppermint, is the mint most people think of as "mint." It's the mint used in juleps, sauces, and jellies, and it is useful chiefly for these purposes. It does have some effect as a gas reliever, stimulant, and antispasmodic, but to a lesser degree than peppermint.

Spearmint grows in erect, unbranched plants rising as high as 3 feet. It has smooth, bright green leaves with unevenly toothed margins. The flowers, which appear in July or August, vary from almost white to a deep purple and are clustered on a single flower spike. Spearmint is most easily differentiated from peppermint by its taste and by the lack of down on the leaves. It is cultivated in much the same way as peppermint.

The apple mint, *M. rotundifolia,* is often found hanging about dumps, compost heaps, and waste places. It is a small, unassuming plant, not difficult to please as to sun or shade and soil fertility. It has soft, gray-green woolly leaves, somewhat round, as its specific name suggests, and gray-white blossoms, shading to pink or pale purple.

Pennyroyal, *M. pulegium,* is treated in a separate entry, later in this chapter.

Bergamot or orange mint, *M. citrata,* is notable for its distinctive, citruslike fragrance. Its rounded, broad leaves are dark green with a hint of purple. The undersides of the leaves often have a reddish hue, and in the spring the entire plant is distinctly reddish purple. Easily cultivated, it adds an interesting fragrance to the herb garden, and, harvested, to tea-time and potpourris.

## Oregano

Oregano is a mystery of the herb world. There is no agreement as to which species of the genus *Origanum* is referred to by the common name oregano. Some growers say oregano is *O. heracleoticum,* while a number of other authorities refer to *O. vulgare* as oregano. Still a third group of authorities cites the two species without attaching the common name oregano to either; these authorities call *O. heracleoticum* winter marjoram and *O. vulgare* wild marjoram. The two plants, though of the same genus, are quite different.

*O. heracleoticum* is a perennial native to Greece and Cyprus. It isn't fully acclimated to harsh winters, so in the northern areas of the United States it should be treated as a tender perennial. A dense system of fine roots produces a low-growing, almost creeping plant with very hairy leaves. The flower stalks grow erect, about 12 inches tall, and develop at their ends small clusters of white flowers. The seeds are light brown and tiny.

*O. vulgare* is also a perennial, also a native of the Mediterranean. It, however, is quite hardy. The plant is erect, rising to 2 feet in height. It has dull, gray-green, oval leaves, far less hairy than those of *O. heracleoticum*. The flowers can be pink, white, purple, or lilac.

Oregano is, of course, famous as a seasoning, primarily due to its use on pizza, in spaghetti sauce, and in other tomato dishes. Sparingly add the leaves, fresh or dried, to any of these dishes. Oregano is also a flavorful garnish for beef or lamb stews, gravies, soups, salads, or tomato juice.

*O. vulgare* has an ancient medicinal reputation, the Greeks having used it both internally and externally. Herbalists have noted that its warming qualities have made it useful as a liniment. A frequently mentioned toothache remedy is oregano oil. The ancient Greeks made warm poultices of the leaves to apply to painful swellings.

Because of the strong balsamitic odor of the whole plant, it has had some use in potpourris, sachets, and aromatic waters, although it takes a secondary role to sweet marjoram in such applications.

Oregano can be started from seed or cuttings. The real trick seems to be getting the seed or cutting from a true oregano plant. In any case, the plant is easily started.

Oregano needs only modest soil fertility, though good drainage and tilth are essential. Planting outside with a distance of 12 inches between plants should be delayed until danger of frost has passed. Hoeing and weed control are important; mulching with cocoa hulls or hay helps to keep the plants clean. Water requirements are minimal, generally supplied by average rainfall.

As soon as the white flowers appear, oregano is ready for harvest, unless of course, continued picking for fresh use during its growth never allows it to flower. Even then oregano should be trimmed about six weeks after planting, cutting off all shoots to within 1 inch from the growing center. This practice stimulates dense, bushy growth.

In addition to inside drying, oregano is one of the few herbs which may be dried outside in the sun after harvesting without losing its properties. It dries very fast due to its "hot" nature. Rubbing the dried material through a fine screen will prepare the oregano for culinary use.

## Parsley

One of the best known herbs, parsley is also one of the most effective and versatile. Mostly used as a decorative herb, it has high nutritional and medicinal value which is unfortunately overlooked.

Parsley is believed to be indigenous to Sardinia, Turkey, Algeria, and Lebanon, where it still grows wild. The Romans are credited for bringing the herb to England, and the English carried it and cultivated it throughout the world.

It is a rich source of calcium, thiamine, riboflavin, and niacin. It abounds in vitamin A, and has more vitamin C than oranges. Because of its richness in vitamins, some consider it excellent to ease the pain of arthritis. Parsley is also useful for eliminating bad breath.

In the first year, the biennial herb develops a multitude of green leaves on long stems until the winter halts its growth. White roots of various thicknesses, depending on variety, penetrate the soil to a depth of a foot. Flower stalks, reaching a height of over 3 feet, develop the second year, with greenish yellow flowers on clusters of umbels. The seeds are grayish brown and germinate within three weeks.

Since the herb gardener is generally interested only in the leaves, parsley is usually planted each year and considered as an annual. It doesn't transplant well, and so should be planted outside.

Traditionally, parsley is planted in rows where it forms an attractive border to a garden. Early and shallow seeding will aid successful germination, even without watering.

The best type of soil for parsley is fertile and humusy with good moisture-holding capacity. Well-rotted compost is excellent fertilizing material, worked into the soil with a hoe or by rototilling. Avoid fresh manure, however, because it will attract flies and could result in the infestation of maggots.

Weed control is especially important with parsley because it develops so slowly at first. It's a good idea to hoe around the herb on a weekly basis until a hay or straw mulch takes over control of the weeds.

Because parsley is primarily used fresh, it is usually picked almost daily in the summer months. The larger outer leaves should be cut or broken first, always close to the core of the plant, without leaving parts of stems attached. Parsley can also be harvested by cutting the whole plant about an inch above the ground. Be sure not to damage the growing point, however.

The harvested plant should be dried in its entirety in the shade, in a short time. It may be necessary to finish the drying in the oven. Once dried, parsley should be crushed and stored in a tight container. Keep it away from moist places.


## Pennyroyal

There are two pennyroyals, an American pennyroyal and an English pennyroyal, which appear to have little in common, yet their utilitarian characteristics are very much the same.

The English pennyroyal has the better standing in the herbal literature, since it emanates from the right part of the world for that. But the American pennyroyal probably has as long a history of use, by the Indians and later by the settlers.

American pennyroyal is a purely American plant, found from the Atlantic coast west through the Dakotas and south to Texas and Florida. It is a branched annual, growing about a foot tall. Like all the mints, it has a square stem with tiny opposite leaves. Tiny flowers bloom in the leaf axils.

Its minty smell earned it the name "smelling weed" among the Onondagas. Because it was a common plant in most regions of North America, it was familiar to a great many Indian tribes, and a variety of uses were recorded.

The most obvious tie with English pennyroyal is American pennyroyal's unofficial property as an insect repellent. The Indians and settlers alike rubbed their exposed skin with a handful of crushed pennyroyal leaves to protect themselves from the stings and bites of mosquitoes and gnats. It was this quality in English pennyroyal that earned it its common name (the plant's former common name, Pulioll-royall, came from *pulex,* Latin for flea), and the settlers undoubtedly tied its name to the American plant which had the same smell and properties.

English pennyroyal is an official member of the mint family, being of the genus *Mentha* (which American pennyroyal is not). It is a totally insignificant plant, staying low, creeping along the ground. Only the lavender-blossomed flower stalk rises above the ground. The leaves are tiny.

Very early on, English pennyroyal was noticed because it seemed to have the power to drive away fleas.

English pennyroyal is not a native of England, despite its name, but rather a native of the Near East, from where it spread across the cooler parts of Europe and north to Finland. Both the Greeks and the Romans used and valued the little herb, and Pliny, for example, listed a considerable number of disorders pennyroyal was said to remedy.

Both American and English pennyroyal are inhabitants of the

herb garden, though the former is a common wild plant in most areas of the United States. It can be found in spots with dry, acid soil and full sun. The garden conditions should duplicate, as well as possible, the natural conditions American pennyroyal likes.

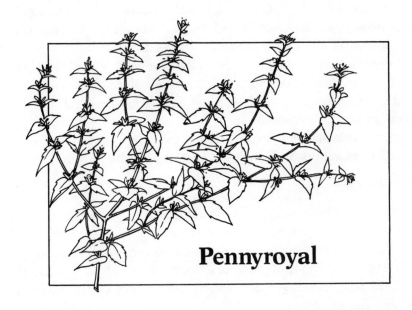

**Pennyroyal**

Sewn into sachets or bags, dried pennyroyal leaves are said to make an effective natural moth repellent.

Since it is an annual, it must be started from seed. The seeds are slow to germinate, but once the plant is established, maintaining it should be no problem, as it self-sows freely.

English pennyroyal may be started from seed, which germinates in the dark at a temperature of 65° to 70°F, but it is slow to germinate and takes a long time to establish itself. English pennyroyal, as a perennial, is best started from cuttings or root divisions. It roots very easily provided it's kept moist enough at all times. As the pennyroyal creeps on the ground, it forms roots wherever the stem touches the ground, which makes it rather easy to subdivide an older plant and make new plants.

The growing of pennyroyal is similar to that of any other mint. It likes a rich soil and will grow in the shade. The plant will thrive on a good water supply and especially a high humus content in the soil. If the humus condition is poor, pennyroyal will develop a light green, yellowish appearance and look starved. Thus, the application of good manure compost is most important. Harvesting of pennyroyal is harder than that of many other plants because the plant grows so low and because the leaves are so small.

The plant should be used fresh as long as it is available, but can also be dried in the shade, preferably before chopping. The dried herb should be stored, as should all dried herbs, in tightly sealed, nonmetallic containers.

Sown into sachets and fragrant bags, either of the pennyroyals will repel moths and lend your clothing a minty aroma.

## Rosemary

Rosemary is used as a medicinal and culinary herb, and it's a beautifully decorative addition to any garden.

The most common variety, *Rosmarinus officinalis,* is a perennial evergreen shrub that grows to a height of 2 to 4 feet. A native of the Mediterranean, rosemary sometimes reaches 6 feet in warm climates and good soil.

Rosemary can be started by seeding, cuttings, or layering. Seeding usually is avoided because of the low percentage of germination. Commonly only one to five of every ten seeds planted will germinate. And it may take up to three years to produce a cuttable bush from seed.

Cuttings are sprouted by taking a 6-inch end tip of new growth and burying its lower 4 inches in sand or vermiculite, or in soil along a shady border of the garden. August is the best time. If the cuttings are planted outside, cover each one with an inverted water glass. They'll be ready to transplant in two to three months.

To layer new sprouts, just weight one or two of the lower branches of a mature bush beneath the soil.

Rosemary will develop into a highly ornamental bush with a

woody stem and boughs of evergreen needles that are dark green on top and lighter on the undersides. Blue flowers, light to dark, form at the tips of branches in the spring.

Rosemary flourishes with occasional watering although it requires well-drained, slightly alkaline soil. It cannot stand to be dehydrated, and that danger especially exists indoors.

A word of caution to growers north of Virginia: rosemary cannot tolerate heavy frosts. It can be left outside year round, but it must be protected. Plant it along the south face of a wall where plastic or glass winter greenhouses can be constructed around the plant. Burlap or a bushel basket can be substituted if necessary. Plants also can be brought inside for the winter, but then care must be taken to supply enough room and enough moisture for the roots. Mist the branches with water every few days, too.

Rosemary prefers sunny or semishady locations.

It's uncertain how rosemary was dispersed from its Mediterranean homeland. One theory holds that Roman conquerors brought it to northern Europe and England with them. Another says the Crusaders brought it home after adopting it from their Saracen foes, who used it as a balm for their wounds.

European herbalists quickly bestowed on rosemary a reputation for the ability to strengthen the memory. That attribute, no doubt, gave rise to the use of rosemary as a symbol for constancy. Rosemary sprigs, dipped in scented water, were woven into bridal bouquets or exchanged by the newlyweds as a token of their troth. Or, richly gilded and bound in multicolored ribbons, the sprigs were presented to the wedding guests as reminders of virtuous fidelity.

Tea is made by infusing a pint of water with 1 ounce of young rosemary tips or a heaping teaspoon of dried leaves. Taken with the juice of half a lemon and a touch of honey, the tea is said to alleviate headaches and help the restless to sleep.

A pleasant sachet and insect-chaser can be made from equal parts of rosemary, lavender, and ground lemon peel.

For a pleasant mouthwash, infuse ⅓ teaspoon each of rosemary, anise, and mint in a cup of water.

It hardly needs to be mentioned that rosemary has a major place in the modern kitchen as a tangy herb to flavor beef and veal, pork, lamb, poultry, soups, stuffings, sauces, and salad dressings. It can be purchased in the form of dried and chopped leaves. But if it is available fresh, cuttings from the new growth can be laid directly on roasts and poultry to add garnish as well as flavor.

## Sage

Sage enjoyed widespread popularity as a virtual panacea for all ailments of the body when herbal medicine was practiced universally.

Fortunately, the decline of herbal medicine didn't leave this pleasant herb in present-day obscurity, for as the medicinal use of sage waned, its role in cookery increased.

The generic name *Salvia* means "health" or "salvation." The specific name *officinalis* indicates that sage was among herbs of medicinal value listed in the official pharmacopoeia. Indeed, sage was listed officially in both England and America.

A Mediterranean native, sage was scattered throughout Europe in the back sacks of Roman legionnaires. Centuries later, when East-West trade developed, European sage became a highly prized export item that was worth three or four times its weight in Chinese tea.

It was, and is, a popular plant. In reality, there are more than a dozen varieties of sage with varying colorations, leaf shapes, and life cycles. *S. officinalis*, being the most popular, is the one discussed here.

Even *S. officinalis* will vary in coloring and leaf markings from plant to plant. The typical *S. officinalis* is a foot or more high with a squarish stem and rounded oblong leaves supported by short stems. Purplish flowers appear in August in whorls at the upper end of the plant. The leaves and stems are coated with stubbly silver-gray hair that has earned the plant the Arabic nickname of "camel's tongue."

Sage is a hardy perennial that will withstand most winters throughout the United States, but it should not be allowed to live beyond three or four years because of the tendency of its stems to become woody and tough. Each spring, the woody growth should be trimmed away. Sage is easy to start from seed because the seeds are large and can be spaced and observed well in their early growth. Indoor seeding will get the plants started four weeks earlier than outdoor planting. Place seeds a foot apart in March for inside planting, or in April outside.

Decisive factors are a sunny, wind-protected area with neutral soil, a good calcium supply, and plenty of moisture, especially in the early stages. Compost can be applied, but fresh manure should be avoided because it produces an undesirable flavor in the herb.

Because sage likes a well-aerated soil, early spring hoeing and cultivation are important. Use cocoa hulls for summer mulch.

Crucial factors in determining how sage will fare over the winter are how the last fall harvesting is accomplished, and when. It should be no later than September, and only leaves and stems high up on the plant should be taken. A light September harvest is all that will be possible the first year. In subsequent years, at least two cuttings will be available.

Dry the leaves in the shade until they're crisp. For tea, just break them up by hand. For seasoning, rub them through a fine screen. The flavor keeps well after drying.

Experts on companion planting suggest placing sage near rosemary. They say the two herbs stimulate one another. Sage also will protect cabbage from its insect enemies and make it more digestible. Young cucumber and grass shoots, however, are inimical to sage and their growth could be stunted by a nearby sage bush.

A strong distillate of sage tea is used to heal brushburns and as a tinting agent to darken graying hair. And sage, rubbed daily on the teeth, is said to keep them sparkling white.

Use finely crushed sage leaves to flavor cheeses and to sprinkle over buttered bread. Use this herb also to flavor sausages, fowl, and pork; one of its properties is that sage aids the digestibility of heavy, greasy meats.

Use it sparingly at first because it has a heavy, almost domi-
nating flavor. To tone sage down, some cooks say that parsley added
in large measure to the sage will take the edge off its pungency.

For a unique after-dinner mint, brush egg white diluted with a
bit of water over fresh sage leaves. Sprinkle powdered sugar lightly
over the leaves. In addition to making an interesting light dessert,
the sage mints will bring the herb's gas-relieving property to the
aid of distressed diners.

## Summer Savory

Summer savory is by far the most popular of more than a
dozen different species of the aromatic *Satureia* genus.

A hardy annual whose growth tends toward a symmetrical
ordering of branches, summer savory can be grown equally well
outdoors, where it reaches 18 inches, or indoors where it will be
somewhat smaller. Now used almost exclusively in the kitchen,
summer savory nonetheless is a member of that herbal group that
was held to have medicinal properties in the days when medicine
conjured images of steaming infusions and mealy poultices.

Summer savory makes a delightful tea. Make it in the usual
fashion of infusing 1 ounce of the herb in 1 pint of boiled water.
Add 1½ tablespoons to ¼ pound of butter for a tangy spread. Egg
dishes profit by the addition of summer savory, and so do nearly all
kinds of meat, fowl, and green salads.

The ancient Romans used summer savory or flavor vinegar.
Virgil, renowned as a beekeeper as well as a poet, made sure his
hives had easy access to the herb, for it enhanced the honey.

Roots of the summer savory bush are well divided and spread
laterally through the upper layer of soil. They produce a plant that
is equally well branched above ground, with leaves that are dark
green and have the shape of wide needles a ½ inch long. It flowers
in July, producing light pink to violet flowers in the leaf axils in
little bunches of up to five flowers. The nut-shaped seeds are dark
brown to black; they germinate in two or three weeks when exposed

to light. Their viability decreases rapidly after the first year.

Savory is best sown directly in outside rows 9 inches to a foot apart, or broadcast and later thinned. Shallow seeding—not deeper than ⅛ inch—is important for proper germination. If topsoil dries out quickly, water the seedbed lightly to keep it moist. Water after sunset to avoid crusting of the topsoil.

Savory is a fast-growing herb that will shade the soil in a short time and so act as its own mulch. Special care should be taken, though, to keep the soil weed-free in its early growth. Weeding can become very difficult if weeds are allowed to develop and tangle themselves around summer savory's early growth. Slight hilling will help to keep the plants upright.

Dwarfed or slow growth will most likely be due to one thing: a lack of water. Savory's moisture requirements are very high, so be sure to keep it moist during dry weather. Indoor pots of summer savory should be misted at least twice a week. Moderate fertilization is sufficient, for savory prefers a soil that is light and only moderately nutritious. Avoid fresh manure.

Experts on companion planting have noted that summer savory aids onions in their growth, so it makes a pleasant as well as a useful border around them. It also makes a beneficial neighbor to green beans, both in the garden and in the cooking pot.

Harvesting may begin as soon as the plants are 6 inches high, and it may continue all summer. The object is to prevent summer savory from flowering, after which leaves will curl and turn yellow and brown. Early harvesting should take just the tops of the plants. The main harvest, done when the plant insists on flowering, should be made as soon as the flowers open. The whole plant should be taken and dried.

Drying savory takes little time. Spread the whole plant on a fine screen or on paper and allow it to dry in warm shade. In a climate with low humidity, especially at night, the savory could even be dried outside in the sun, provided the drying would be complete within two days. The leaves also can be frozen, but they dry well.

# Tarragon

Tarragon is one of the handful of herbs that has passed down to us from antiquity. Like basil, rosemary, sage, and thyme, tarragon traces its historic roots back hundreds of years before Christ.

Its use was recorded by the Greeks about 500 B.C.; tarragon was among the so-called "simples"—one-remedy herbs—used by Hippocrates. European gardeners knew tarragon in the Middle Ages, but it wasn't until the end of those dark times that it leaped the English Channel. It entered England during the Tudor reign, probably as a preferred gift for the royal herb garden from a Continental monarch. For many years, tarragon was relatively unknown outside the royal garden. It must eventually have made good its escape, though, because it arrived on America's post-Revolutionary shores in the first few years of the nineteenth century.

In the kitchen, tarragon has a wide range of uses that begins with the traditional tarragon vinegar. This best-known of tarragon elixirs can be made simply by filling a wide-mouthed bottle with fresh sprigs, then soaking them in fine-quality vinegar of white wine. A delicate-flavored vinegar is important so as not to stifle tarragon's relatively light flavor.

Next to other herbs, however, tarragon can be overpowering. It should be used with discretion in combination with its sisters.

Considered to be one of the fine herbs, as opposed to the robust herbs, tarragon makes a delicious addition to all kinds of white sauces, fish, cheese, eggs, and green vegetables such as spinach, peas, and lima beans. Cauliflower benefits from a sprinkle of tarragon, and as an ingredient of tartar sauce, the herb is indispensable.

Try this for a heavenly light lunch: to your favorite recipe for creamy white sauce, add parsley and tarragon. Serve it over poached eggs nestled in shells of the lightest pastry. Accompany with a chilled, light, dry white wine.

When it comes time to acquire your first tarragon bush, beware! There are two distinct varieties, and some herb houses don't differentiate. One is desirable, and that's the one we've been talking about. It's commonly called German or French tarragon. Unless you have access to an established bush from which you can take a slip or some roots, you'll have to buy the bush from a commercial herb house. The European variety rarely produces fertile flowers that go to seed.

The other variety is the less desirable Eastern variety, commonly called Russian tarragon. It does not seem to have a separate specific name, but it differs greatly from the Western variety. Russian tarragon produces seeds copiously and seems more vigorous a plant than the aromatic European variety, but it's unfortunately lacking in the oils that make European tarragon such a delight to taste and smell.

A good rule of thumb is just to avoid buying tarragon seed; start your plant from a cutting or root division. The cuttings can be taken early in the spring, after the main plant has begun to show new growth. Place the new slip under an inverted water glass to keep it warm. Keep the plants about 20 inches apart because tarragon sends out a lateral root structure rather than a vertical one.

Tarragon likes moderate sun in a fertile, well-drained location. Heavy mulching is advisable to improve the soil's capacity to hold moisture, although a thoroughly wet soil won't do.

Fertilize established plants with a liquid solution such as fish emulsion after taking cuttings.

Root division can be done likewise in March or April by dividing the root cluster of a single mature plant into two or three clumps. Mature plants should be divided every four years to rejuvenate them. It would be a wise idea to set up a rotation system for dividing some plants each year if you plan to make tarragon a mainstay of your herb garden.

Be very careful if you choose to hoe your tarragon; the bushes' lateral, shallow root structure makes them vulnerable.

With good care, tarragon in the garden will grow to 2 or 3 feet. Upright green stalks will carry elongated green or dark green leaves. Small yellow and black flowers form in August.

Harvest tarragon when the lower leaves start to turn yellow. This yellowing is a sign either of insufficient fertilization or of aging. In either case, the yellowed leaves will not turn green again, and that's cause enough to gather them before the discoloration progresses. Leave 2 or 3 inches of stem.

First cuttings, however, may be taken as early as June. Older plants are more likely to give a heavy first cutting and second, or even third, crops.

Tarragon leaves brown easily, so dry them carefully to avoid that. Strip them from the stem and dry in a warm, dry, shaded, and well-ventilated area. The temperature should not exceed 90°F.

When the leaves are dry, seal them in tight, dry containers; they'll reabsorb moisture at the first chance.

Tarragon winters well if its beds are covered with straw or hay to protect the roots slightly. Consider, though, that taking one or two plants inside for the winter will grace your home with the sweet aroma of fresh-mown hay all winter long.

After the last fall cutting, transplant a tarragon root cluster into a pot no less than 10 inches in diameter. Leave plenty of room for those roots to spread out. If the potting soil is not sandy, add some light gravel for airiness.

Don't overwater tarragon indoors. It should be allowed to dry out for a day or two before rewatering. Twice-monthly feedings will make it thrive.

## Thyme

Another of the herbs whose beginnings go back two millennia or more, thyme has acquired such a wide usefulness both medicinally and in cooking that it is a mainstay of the modern herbal array.

Traditionally, thyme has been graced with many strong positive associations, not the least of which has been humor. In Renaissance England, when wits were keen and words well chosen, it was said that thyme could hardly enter a conversation between two persons of quick mind without a welter of puns developing. The first allusion to the herb soon became jokingly known as "punning thyme."

From the earliest, thyme has been associated with honey, without doubt because it attracts bees in great profusion. It's common practice in Mediterranean orchards to plant thyme as a groundcover that also attracts pollinating insects to the fruit trees.

Young sheep in the plant's native Mediterranean region often are set out to graze on fields of wild thyme, a feed that many believe enhances the flavor of lamb.

The bee-honey-thyme image lasted through the centuries and bloomed in the European age of chivalry, when thyme flourished as a symbol of strength, activity, and bravery. Many a lady embroidered her knight a pennant showing a bee hovering over a sprig of thyme.

Thyme's generic name *Thymus* is thought by many lexicographers to be a derivation of the Greek *thumus* ("courage"). Others believe it evolved from an ancient Greek expression meaning "to fumigate." Thyme was considered to have strong antiseptic properties, and it was used as an incense to purify the air. A similar belief was that a hillside of thyme not only sweetened the air near it, but cleansed it of bad vapors as well.

In the kitchen, dried thyme leaves are as nearly universal a seasoning as any herb could be. One recent expert on herbal cookery advocated using thyme "as freely as salt — in other words, in practically everything." It's pleasing in red meat, poultry, and fish as well as almost any vegetable, even the heartier ones.

Botanically, there are many closely related species in the *Thymus* genus. Most of them bear a close resemblance to *T. vulgaris,* a species that itself has at least three varieties: English thyme, German winter thyme, and French summer thyme. They differ mainly in the appearance of their leaves, being respectively variegated, broad, and narrow.

The different varieties of thyme also are grouped generally into upright and trailing types with *T. vulgaris* being the most common of the uprights and wild thyme *(T. serpyllum)* being foremost among the creeping thymes that make so pleasant a groundcover.

*T. vulgaris,* common thyme, is usually started from seed although cuttings or root divisions can be substituted. Seeding should be done in indoor flats because a temperature of around 70°F—unlikely outside in the spring—is needed for germination. The seeds are exceptionally small; it takes some 170,000 to make an ounce. They should be evenly distributed over the seedbed, and covered only lightly or not at all. They usually germinate in about two weeks.

After the young plants have taken root, they can be moved outdoors to cooler weather. They should be set 9 inches apart in full sun in a sandy, dry soil that is moderately fertilized. Thyme's nutrient requirements are not heavy; most important is to avoid heavy, wet soils.

A dense system of fine roots will develop, along with a well-branched surface structure of woody stems and branches to which are attached small oval-shaped leaves. The plant will reach 8 to 10 inches in height. Leaves will be gray-green, and pink or violet flowers will appear in the leaf axils of the tip ends from May to August.

Weed control is important because weeds can be a debilitating competitor for nutrients with the small, slow-developing young thyme. Once the shoots are established, mulching will hold soil warmth and discourage weed rivals.

Open cultivation and hoeing always should be avoided around low herbs because the hoeing and the rain's action on the bare earth will dirty the lower branches of the plant.

Harvest thyme just before flowers begin to open by cutting the entire plant 1½ or 2 inches from the ground. A second growth will develop, although that should not be cut at all. Harvesting the second growth will reduce thyme's winter hardiness, especially if the ground is bare and the temperatures fluctuate widely. If you must have more thyme late in the summer, prune just the upper third of the plant, and then be sure to give it extra attention in the cold months.

Thyme, especially if a second growth is taken, should be mulched or covered over with an earthen blanket for the winter. Like all members of the thyme genus, common thyme is a hardy perennial but it needs care over the winter to survive the cold months.

After harvesting, lay the entire plant on a fine screen or a sheet of newspaper and dry it in the warm shade. When dried, the leaves will separate from the woody stems upon light rubbing. Throw the stems onto the compost pile; the leaves alone are usable. Drying is easy, and thyme stores well at low humidity.

If you move your thyme bed to another corner of the garden, be sure to fertilize the plant's old area heavily before planting another herb there. Thyme tends to rob the soil of nutrients.

## Yarrow

If you were a twelfth-century knight at arms, you'd probably carry a pouch of fresh yarrow leaves with you as nature's own first-aid kit. But being a twentieth-century gardener, you'll undoubtedly want to turn to yarrow instead as a wonderfully decorative border around your garden.

Despite the plant's principal use now for its bright, long-blooming flowers, there are still several practical reasons for cultivating yarrow. In companion planting with other medicinal herbs, yarrow—like its cousin tansy—repels Japanese beetles, ants, and flies. In addition, its tonic and astringent properties justify its place in the herbal medicine chest even to this day.

Yarrow gets its generic name *Achillea* from the legend that comrades of the Greek hero Achilles used yarrow to heal their wounds during the Trojan War. The specific name *millefolium* derives from yarrow's feathery leaves, so well divided the plant appears to be thousand-leaved.

Yarrow is a hardy perennial that grows wild and will exist—though maybe not thrive—in almost any grade of soil. It's considered, with some justification, to be a weed by many gardeners.

The flowers of the yarrow plant lend themselves to drying for bouquets. You can choose from among white, red, orange, and yellow blooming varieties although the white and red seem to be most important and most often cultivated for medicinal and culinary use. Orange and yellow are grown more for their floral attributes.

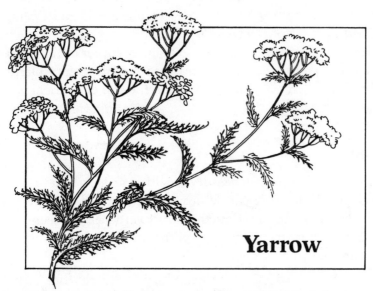

**Yarrow**

Yarrow makes a wonderfully decorative border around your garden.

A word of caution when using the white medicinal variety. This variety must be moved annually because it excretes a toxin to the soil that eventually will defeat even its own growth. If you need to have the white medicinal type, you might grow it for a season — just long enough to get to know and recognize the plant. Then hunt it wild; it flourishes unattended in almost any area of the eastern United States.

Starting yarrow can be done either from seed or by dividing the root clumps of established plants. Yarrow seed will germinate in light. Sow it on top of fine soil and keep it moist until it germinates. Start it indoors in March so it will be ready for harvesting in June or July. Although fertilization is of minor importance because of yarrow's hardiness, annual applications of bonemeal will promote its growth. Too, yarrow will produce a more pleasing aroma in light, sandy soils than in heavy, clay ones.

For medicinal and culinary uses, cut the whole plant at the peak of the flowering. Chop the stem and leaves and dry them rapidly in temperatures of 90° to 100°F. Because of their fine division, yarrow leaves will darken quickly if not dried rapidly and thoroughly.

Yarrow used as a companion plant will drive away many common garden insects, and will increase the content of volatile oils in nearby herbs.

As a general tonic, yarrow is said to have a salutary effect on the entire nervous system. Throughout the centuries the herb has been used also as snuff, a toothache remedy, and as a substitute for hops in the brewing of homemade beer.

In the kitchen, yarrow occupies only a marginal place. Its usefulness is limited to an occasional stand-in for cinnamon or nutmeg.

## Herb Pests

| Pest | Description | Herb(s) Affected | Control |
|---|---|---|---|
| **Aphid** (*Aphis, Macrosiphum, Myzus* spp.) (*many other species*) | Soft-bodied, pear-shaped insect less than $\frac{1}{10}$ in. long; may have clear wings or be wingless; green to bluish black DAMAGE: insect pierces plant tissue and extracts sap; transmits viral diseases; leaves turn yellow | Caraway, chervil, and oregano | Foil mulch; insecticidal soap spray; diatomaceous earth or rotenone dusts; ladybugs; lacewings; syrphid flies |
| **Carrot weevil** (*Listronotus oregonensis*) | Brownish insect, $\frac{1}{3}$ in. long with hard shell; pale, legless, brown-headed larva DAMAGE: larva tunnels into herb's top and root, destroying most of plant's tissue | Parsley | Crop rotation; clean cultivation |
| **Japanese beetle** (*Popillia japonica*) | Shiny metallic green beetle with copper brown wings, about $\frac{1}{2}$ in. long; larva is inch-long white grub DAMAGE: adult eats leaves, resulting in lacy skeletons of veining, as well as flowers; grub feeds on roots and underground stems | Basil | Milky spore disease (*Bacillus popilliae*); fall tiphia (*Tiphia popilliavora*) |
| **Leaf miner** (*Liriomyza* spp.) | Small, black fly, usually with yellow stripes; tiny yellowish larva DAMAGE: maggot feeds between upper and lower leaf surfaces, causing white tunnels or blotches on leaves | Oregano | Remove and destroy affected leaves before maggots mature; cover plants with screening to prevent infestations |

| Pest | Description | Herb(s) Affected | Control |
|------|-------------|------------------|---------|
| **Mealybug** (*Pseudococcus* spp.) | Yellowish wingless female covered with dense white cottony powder; ⅒ in. long; male is tiny fly. DAMAGE: feeds by sucking sap; secretes honeydew, which attracts ants and promotes sooty mold | Rosemary | Insecticidal soap spray; swabbing with alcohol; knocking off with a strong stream of water; mealybug destroyer *Cryptolaemus montrouzieri*; green lacewing larvae |
| **Mint flea beetle** (*Longitarsus menthaphagus*) | Small, dark, oval beetle that jumps vigorously when disturbed; tiny white larva. DAMAGE: adult eats tiny rounded holes in leaves, so foliage looks riddled; larva feed on plant roots | Mints | Lime, diatomaceous earth, or rotenone dusts; keep weeds out of garden and vicinity; cover seedbeds with gauze or Reemay |
| **Parsley worm** (*Papilio polyxenes asterius*) | Green caterpillar 2 in. long; has yellow-dotted black band across each segment; larva of the black swallowtail butterfly. DAMAGE: feeds on parsley leaves | Parsley | Handpicking; Bt (*Bacillus thuringiensis*) |
| **Root-knot nematode** (*Meloidogyne* spp.) | Microscopic worm with pearly egg masses. DAMAGE: stimulates injured plant tissue to form galls, which block the flow of water and nutrients to the plant, leading to stunting, wilt, and yellowing; roots appear scabby | Lavender and parsley | Add organic matter to encourage parasitic fungi; plant rotation; monocropping with marigolds |

*(continued)*

## Herb Pests — *Continued*

| Pest | Description | Herb(s) Affected | Control |
|------|-------------|------------------|---------|
| **Scale** (Coccideae) | Legless, wingless female ⅕–1¹⁄₁₂ in. long, covered with a waxy or cottony substance; male may have pair of wings DAMAGE: feeds by sucking sap, causing stunting and chlorosis; honeydew secretions attract ants and promote sooty mold | Bay and rosemary | Insecticidal soap spray |
| **Slug** (*Limax maximus*) (*Deroceras reticulatum*) (*many other species*) | Grayish or grayish brown, legless, slimy mollusk, ½–4 in. long, antennae, nocturnal DAMAGE: feeds on foliage, scraping holes in leaves and causing extensive damage | Basil, calendula, and sage | Handpicking; stale beer traps; boards placed in damp areas as traps and checked each morning |
| **Snail** | Gray, pinkish, black, brown, or mottled mollusk, with soft, slimy body and coiled shell, ½–3 in. long, antennae; chiefly nocturnal DAMAGE: same as for slug | Calendula | Handpicking; stale beer traps; diatomaceous earth dusts; copper bands around tops of boards that frame raised beds |
| **Spider mite** (*Tetranychus urticae*) (*many other species*) | Microscopic, 8-legged, often web-spinning arachnid; some 2-spotted; green, yellow, brown, or red DAMAGE: feeds by sucking plant juices; leaves show pinprick spots and puckering; weakens plants | Mints, oregano, rosemary, sage, and thyme | Cold water spray on leaves; insecticidal soap spray; slurry of flour, buttermilk, and water; lacewings, ladybugs, predatory mites *Phytoseiulus persimilis* and *Amblyseium californicus* |

Rodale Press, Inc., publishes RODALE'S ORGANIC GARDENING®,
the all-time favorite gardening magazine.
For information on how to order your subscription,
write to RODALE'S ORGANIC GARDENING®, Emmaus, PA 18098.